£3.50

Da Grann

Biography

Shipwreck Story and the Mutinous Mind Behind The Wager

Janeen Lemons

Table of Contents

Prologue

    Part One: The Wooden World

    Chapter 1: The First Lieutenant

    Chapter 2: A Gentleman Volunteer

    Chapter 3: The Gunner

Part Two: Into the Storm

    Chapter 4: Dead Reckoning

    Chapter 5: The Storm Within the Storm

    Chapter 6: Alone

    Chapter 7: The Gulf of Pain

Part Three: Castaways

    Chapter 8: Wreckage

    Chapter 9: The Beast

    Chapter 10: Our New Town

    Chapter 11: Nomads of the Sea

    Chapter 12: The Lord of Mount Misery

    Chapter 13: Extremities

    Chapter 14: Affections of the People

    Chapter 15: The Ark

    Chapter 16: My Mutineers

Part Four: Deliverance

    Chapter 17: Byron's Choice

    Chapter 18: Port of God's Mercy

Chapter 19: The Haunting

Chapter 20: The Day of Our Deliverance

Part Five: Judgment

Chapter 21: A Literary Rebellion

Chapter 22: The Prize

Chapter 23: Grub Street Hacks

Chapter 24: The Docket

Chapter 25: The Court-Martial

Chapter 26: The Version That Won

Epilogue

Prologue

The sun was the sole impartial witness.

It observed a peculiar, disorganized vessel being forcefully tossed in the South Atlantic, its sails torn to shreds and its timbers warped by storms. The boat, which was little more than a patchwork of scraps and desperation, crept into an inlet along the southeastern coast of Brazil just as it seemed destined to perish against the reef. The villagers observed the men, who were gaunt, skeletal, and scarcely clothed, their bodies having been ravaged by sea and starvation. Certain individuals were unable to endure. Upon his arrival, one individual expired. However, one individual, who was shaking with exertion, was able to stand and speak. He declared that they were survivors of His Majesty's Ship The Wager, a British man-of-war that was believed to have been lost at sea for an extended period.

This is the beginning of the narrative that David Grann was intended to convey.

In this vivid, meticulously researched biography, we follow the renowned author not only throughout his life, but also through his unwavering pursuit of stories that have been interred beneath centuries of silence and imperial myth. Grann's magnum opus, The Wager, is not merely a maritime adventure; it is an exploration of moral collapse, human endurance tested in the most unforgiving regions of existence, and the political apparatus that influences the narratives we accept.

In September 1740, The Wager departed from Portsmouth as part of a British squadron on a clandestine expedition to capture a Spanish galleon that was laden with treasure—"the prize of all the oceans." However, the squadron was engulfed by a tempest in a location near the dreaded Cape Horn, off the coast of South America. The wager disappeared. It was presumed that all individuals aboard—approximately 250 men—had perished.

However, a fragment of the ship's crew resurfaced 283 days after the ship was last observed. They had traversed nearly three thousand miles in a handmade boat, enduring tidal surges, freezing storms, and earthquakes. They were praised as champions and discussed the importance of leadership, providence, and courage. However, six months later, an additional vessel—smaller, more dilapidated, and carrying even more destitute survivors—washed up on the Chilean coast. And their account completely upended everything.

These individuals asserted that the so-called martyrs were mutineers.

The narrative abruptly fragmented. England was inundated with competing pamphlets, as each faction sought to influence public opinion and evade retribution. Mutiny was a capital offense. A narrative that fails could result in execution. The truth was evasive, despite the Admiralty's convening of a court-martial to uncover it. Starvation had deprived the men of civilization on the desolate island where the shipwrecked crew once held to life. Factions were established. Dissolution of the naval organization. Murders were muttered. A number of outposts were constructed and subsequently abandoned. Men disappeared during the night. And beneath it all, an unspoken horror persisted—it is possible that some of the men consumed the deceased.

David Grann, who is preoccupied with precision, empathy, and the ambiguous spaces where history merges with myth, reconstructs this event not only as a chronicler of facts, but also as a storyteller with a moral compass. He follows the psychological disintegration of leaders, the betrayal of ideals, the descent from command to chaos, and the fragile human attempts to impose meaning on catastrophe. In the process, he reveals the personal cost of imperial ambition and the significant fallacy of moral clarity during periods of collapse.

This biography follows Grann's life as it follows his evolving body of work, which includes The Lost City of Z and Killers of the Flower Moon. It culminates in The Wager, a masterpiece of historical narrative that merges disaster, survival, mutiny, and memory into a single, sweeping narrative. His work is a testament to the influence of stories on fate, particularly when the stakes are life and death, justice and obliteration.

The biography of David Grann: Shipwrecked Story and the Mutinous Mind Behind The Wager is not only a portrait of a man, but also a reflection on the agonizing cost of being believed, truth, and history.

------- * * * -------

Part One
The Wooden World

Chapter 1
THE FIRST LIEUTENANT

In addition to a sea container, each member of Commodore George Anson's squadron carried a shadow. The stories that lie beneath each uniform are too weighty to mention: debts that tarnished reputations, affairs that soured, inheritances that were denied, secrets that were tucked away in journals or left behind in tearful goodbyes. David Cheap, a burly, haunted Scotsman in his early forties, was among them. His dignity had been bruised by a family inheritance dispute, and his debts threatened to swallow him whole. He had been denied a future by the land. The sea, with its hierarchy, violence, and merciless clarity, offered redemption.

In January 1740, the British Empire was on the brink of a conflict with Spain, its imperial rival, which had been precipitated by the discovery of a severed ear in a jar. The fervor of conquest and the seductive glint of silver from the Americas were the driving forces behind the War of Jenkins' Ear, as it would eventually be dubbed. The greatest aspiration of Britain was to initiate two naval operations against Spanish colonies. George Anson, who was stoic, unreadable, and meticulous, was assigned a smaller, secretive mission to circumnavigate the globe, weaken Spanish Pacific forces, and capture a fabled treasure galleon laden with silver coins and silks from Asia, while Admiral Vernon led the largest amphibious assault in history toward Cartagena.

In his haunting reconstruction of The Wager, David Grann tracks not only the voyage of ships but also the human spirits that are under siege. He follows the narrative from its imperial inception in the fog-shrouded shipyards of Portsmouth, through typhoons off Cape Horn, and into the icy depths of Patagonia, where The Wager, one of the ships in Anson's squadron, met its demise. The subsequent events were not merely catastrophic; they were a precipitous decline.

The survivors, including officers, sailors, and marines, were forced to endure a novel type of test, one that was not influenced by cannon fire but rather by starvation, madness, and cold, after being stranded on a desolate island at the edge of the known world. Authority fractured as discipline disintegrated. Commander David Cheap, who was once a symbol of authority, was gradually dismantled by injury, betrayal, and his own rigidity. A chain of command evolved into a chain of resentment. Factions undergo a division. Murders transpired. Men disappeared into the wilderness. Chaos ensued as naval law fractured. Within that confusion, there were murmurs of cannibalism that drifted on the wind.

On a three-thousand-mile journey through storms, ice, and fire to reach Brazil, eighty-one survivors, clinging to faith and lashed-together planks, attempted the impossible mission. They arrived as spirits, devoid of reason, soaked, and starved, rather than as a crew. However, the narrative did not conclude at that point.

Another triumvirate washed up on the shores of Chile six months later, their bodies consumed by insects and their minds partially shattered by delirium. Additionally, they introduced an alternative narrative that would undermine the falsehood of heroism that had been perpetuated in Brazil. They claimed that the men who had survived The Wager were not valiant loyalists; rather, they were mutineers, deserters, and liars. Therefore, the ultimate journey commenced with the second arrival, not across oceans, but across narratives.

The Admiralty convened a court-martial in England, and Grann follows the return of these rival survivors. Reputations were decimated in that chamber, which was wood-paneled and eerily silent. Pamphlets were published by survivors who accused one another of dereliction, cowardice, and calumnies. Philosophers such as Rousseau, Montesquieu, and Voltaire were struck by the existential implications of the conflicting narratives, which collided with such intensity. What did it mean to remain human in the absence of law? What was the thickness of the veneer of civilization when it was subjected to the elements?

From the perspective of David Grann, a contemporary master of narrative nonfiction, The Wager is transformed into a narrative that not only explores the ill-fated imperial expedition but also the illusions that underpin empires. Grann also recounts the narrative of a nation that is anxious to broaden its influence, disguised as moral obligation, in the process of recounting Cheap's story. In addition to recovering a maritime calamity, he exposes the frailty of order, the psychic wreckage of ambition, and the desperate, dangerous need to be believed by resurrecting The Wager.

This biography delves into the literary development of David Grann, from his early reporting days to the global acclaim of The Lost City of Z and Killers of the Flower Moon, in addition to the uncanny voyage that served as the inspiration for The Wager. He is a unique voice in historical storytelling due to his intuitive comprehension of suspense, his unwavering commitment to the preservation of forgotten truth, and his concern for moral complexity.

David Cheap was a man who was pursuing notoriety and evading a more sinister force. He discovered his redemption on the roiling decks of a man-of-war, rather than in the courts or parishes of the land, as the son of a fractured Scottish family who was denied inheritance and encumbered by debt. The sea served as both a crucible and a cathedral for Cheap. He perceived order in its code. He perceived purpose in its anguish. He envisioned his future ascension to the captaincy and, with any luck, to legend while aboard His Majesty's ship, the Centurion, as it crested on wind and wave.

However, the year was 1740, and the British Empire was in the process of preparing for war. This conflict was partially initiated by the suspension of a severed ear in a jar. London's privileged entertained fantasies of conquest and treasure in response to Spain's new status as an adversary. Silver-laden galleons in the Pacific were the subject of whispers from the Admiralty. George Anson, the taciturn and enigmatic commanding officer of Cheap, had been appointed commodore of a clandestine squadron that was en route to the opposite side of the globe. Their directives were unequivocal: "Destroy, sink, burn, or otherwise remove."

However, they were required to endure the land before they could embark on their voyage.

Cheap's initial battleground was the British dockyards, which were choked with unfinished ships and decayed timbers. Sabotage, shortages, and storms conspired against them. The sails of the Centurion were chewed by rodents, and its hull was infested with shipworms. The ropes were tattered. Masts fractured. Still, the squadron was awaiting parts, paint, and personnel, as every inch of rigging had to be rebuilt. Spain was not the most formidable adversary. There was a delay.

The Wager, a merchant tub that was abruptly converted into a warship, was the bastard of the fleet. She was unable to reach Portsmouth due to her sluggishness in water, her wide girth, and the ominous omens that plagued her. Dandy Kidd, her commander, was a superstitious individual who was purportedly descended from pirates. He harbored fears that she was cursed. However, the Navy had renamed her in honor of Sir Charles Wager, the First Lord of the Admiralty. Consequently, the irony was permanently etched into her hull: they were wagering their lives.

Months have transpired. Canvas and epidermis were penetrated by winter. The Thames became frozen. The squadron was ensnared by politics, indifference, rotted masts, and fractured planks, despite the riverbanks thawing in the spring. By July, nearly nine months had passed without any bloodshed. The entire wrath of the infamous passage, where waves rose as high as buildings, winds screamed without mercy, and daylight vanished into icy fog, would be met if they failed to round Cape Horn before the austral summer concluded.

Cheap was aware of this. Anson was aware of this. However, the Navy's delays did not indicate a retreat.

A man's incomplete narrative was concealed beneath each sail that was extended toward the New World. Some were fleeing from shame. Some individuals pursued prosperity, while others sought to flee. The majority of individuals were unaware of the precise mission's details; they only knew that it involved distant waters and the prospect of a prize that glowed just beyond their grasp. The squadron, when it was ultimately assembled, was not merely an armada; it was a mobile vessel of ambition, secrets, fears, and illusions. Crafted to endure tempests and command oceans, floating wooden fortresses. Alternatively, they were under the impression.

The ships groaned under the weight of rope, livestock, ammunition, and personnel as the squadron finally prepared to depart. Warships that were intended for rapid devastation had evolved into autonomous cities. Under the decks, goats bleated, hogs screamed, and steers—who were coerced to board—refused to walk the gangplanks. Nevertheless, the personnel were still incomplete. The Centurion, the fleet's pride, was devoid of the most critical element: personnel.

This was the world that David Grann resurrects from the dead—not through imagination, but through an unwavering commitment to archival accuracy. Grann unearths the neglected journey that would transform order into anarchy, discipline into depravity in The Wager. The voyage would result in the splintering of ships, the starvation of men on Patagonian islands, and a British court-martial that would be left gasping at the accounts of mutiny, cannibalism, and collapse.

Grann recounts the narrative of not only a catastrophe, but also the moral devastation that results when an empire exceeds its bounds and demands excessively of its soldiers. The tale parallels his own journey from journalist to literary chronicler of history's shadows, which is a quest to understand what men do when the horizon disappears and all that is left is story.

David Cheap had been waiting in the shadow of the Centurion's masts for months, his gaze fixed on a horizon that never seemed to shift, by the time the war was declared. His nerves were gnawed by each delay. The seasons vanished like tidewater, tempers ignited, and supplies rotted. The most significant threat to His Majesty's secret squadron was not Spain or the cannons it would discharge; it was time and the rot that grew in its silence.

This was to be Cheap's most perilous expedition, a three-year imperial wager that necessitated not only the capture of a legendary Spanish treasure galleon, but also amphibious invasions across South America and the Pacific. The design capacity of each vessel, including the Centurion and the Wager that was hastily converted, was to be exceeded. The Wager would transport nearly two hundred and fifty individuals, while the Centurion would transport five hundred. There was no alternative method to defeat the adversary, secure the prize, and return with silver in their possessions and honor surrounding their names.

However, the Navy had exhausted its personnel.

The number of volunteers had diminished. Britain, which was both haughty and stubborn, did not have a conscription system. First Minister Robert Walpole, in a state of rage and desperation, disclosed to Parliament that a third of the Royal Navy's vessels were unusable due to a lack of mariners. "Oh, seamen, seamen, seamen!" he cried, echoing the desperation of a nation that had established its dominion on saltwater and was now paralyzed at the dock.

Cheap pleaded, delayed, and argued. And when the men finally arrived, they were coughing, staggering, and feverish. Their heads were pounding, their joints were throbbing, and a significant number of them were unable to consume sustenance. Some individuals experienced bleeding from the nostril or lapsed into a state of delirium, swatting at ghosts in the air. It was "ship's fever," an invisible horror that was not borne by cannon or saber, but by lice and filth. The disease that modern medicine would refer to as typhus advanced at a rate that exceeded that of any enemy vessel.

More than two hundred individuals contracted illness on the Centurion alone. Before departing the port, over twenty-five individuals perished. Among the vulnerable was Henry, Cheap's own young nephew, who was apprenticed to the sea and was enthusiastic and wide-eyed. Cheap himself acknowledged that he was in a "very indifferent state of health." Nevertheless, they persisted.

The ill were transported to a temporary hospital in Gosport, a converted building that was groaning under the weight of the dying bodies. They were dispersed into taverns and inns throughout the harbor towns when it overflowed, where the aroma of alcohol obliterated any prospect of recovery. They sat in silence, their windows sealed against the cold, three to a cot. One admiral observed, "They die very quickly in this miserable way."

So, the Navy pursued its final option.

The men would be taken if they did not come willingly. The Admiralty unleashed a surge of press gangs, which were armed squads that were authorized to patrol city streets, riverbanks, and seacoasts, seizing any man who exhibited the calloused hands, tar-stained fingers, or sailor's gait of the sea. They referred to it as impressment. Kidnapping was rendered legal in practice.

A gentle touch on the shoulder. A whistle has been sounded. Six men emerged from the shadows and pursued you through alleys, while strangers cursed and spouses screamed. Merchant sailors, watermen, and fishermen—all were considered open game. Even voyagers who had recently returned from years abroad were compelled to disembark before they could embrace their families. In the name of the King, a life was stolen.

Young John Campbell, a merchant sailor, had observed a press crew seize an elderly man on his ship—someone who was trembling and in tears. Campbell moved forward without hesitation. "Please take me instead," he stated. The gang leader, who was amused, nodded. "It is preferable to have a young man with a spirit than a man who is weeping." Campbell was appointed as a midshipman aboard the Centurion after Anson heard the narrative and was impressed. However, not all men experienced the same level of success.

Some seamen managed to escape in disguise, with one individual reportedly donning the cloak, hood, and bonnet of a lady in order to elude his pursuers. Many others either concealed themselves beneath the decks or bribed shipmasters to report them as deceased. Those who were apprehended were escorted onto tenders, which were floating prisons with barred hatches and marines stationed at the stern. Many experienced seasickness as they were jammed together in the darkness. The odor caused some individuals to expire. One survivor recollected, "There was no space to sit or stand apart." A situation that is truly pitiful.

Heartbreak reverberated on the wharves in a manner reminiscent of cannon fire. Families raced to the docks in anticipation of catching a glimpse of a face, a hand, or anything, as they were forewarned by whispers or desperate letters. At Tower Wharf, Samuel Pepys observed as wives screamed their husbands' names, rushed to each group of conscripts arriving, and wept as the ships disappeared down the river. "I was deeply saddened by their words," he wrote.

David Grann, the renowned chronicler of lost histories and moral unravelings, resurrects these human costs not as footnotes to a conflict, but as the very core of The Wager. In his retelling, the voyage to sea is already a descent into a world in which consent is a delusion, disease replaces discipline, and men are stripped of their identity long before they reach the storm-ravaged passage of Cape Horn.

The ports of Portsmouth had become bitter with anticipation by the late summer of 1740. The sailors were ill, the ships were rotting, and David Cheap, who had been once infused with the fervor of purpose, had begun to experience the metallic edge of doubt. He had been pacing the quarterdeck of the Centurion for nearly a year, ensnared in a purgatory of desertion, disease, and delays, rather than at sea.

His directives were unequivocal. The squadron, led by the austere and impenetrable Commodore George Anson, was tasked with the task of sailing into the unknown, crossing the vast Pacific, and capturing a Spanish treasure galleon that was rumored to be "the prize of all the oceans." However, their departure had evolved into a tragic comedy of logistical collapse and imperial arrogance.

The Centurion, like the other ships in the squadron, was designed to operate beyond its intended boundaries. It was originally intended to accommodate 400 individuals; however, it is now capable of accommodating 500. The Wager, a merchant vessel that had been repurposed and was already ungainly, would be occupied by 250 individuals, which is twice her typical complement. However, where were the men?

The volunteers had been patiently awaited by Cheap. The Navy resorted to the old nightmare: the press squad, when they failed to arrive. Numerous individuals were apprehended from taverns, merchant ships, and city streets, with many being apprehended solely on account of the ink stains of tar on their hands. The newly pressed arrived against their will, their eyes sunken with resentment. They fled as soon as they were able.

They disappeared in large numbers. Thirty in a single day from the Severn. A total of over 240 individuals from the entire squadron. A few individuals disappeared from hospitals in Gosport, dragging fevered bodies down alleyways. However, others chose to risk drowning over the certainty of conscription, leaping from tenders into the sea. A man wrote to his wife from the deck of the Centurion, stating, "I would give everything I had if it was a hundred guineas if I could get on shore..." I have no prospects of reaching you. "Do the best you can for the children, and may God bless you and them until I return."

The press groups themselves began to abdicate. One was dispatched by Captain Kidd to locate replacements for the Wager; however, the crew suffered the loss of six members instead.

Cheap, a naval traditionalist, was of the opinion that a sailor must possess "honor, courage... steadiness." In contrast, his observations were revolting. The vessels were not brimming with the courage of the seafaring crew, but rather with the ailing and abandoned. One admiral characterized the recruits as a pandemic in themselves, stating that they were "full of the pox, itch, lame, King's evil... the very filth of London." They were beggars, criminals, and dying men from prison cells and hospital wards. "I have never encountered a group of men who were so badly turned over in any of the previous wars," he wrote. "It is so devastating that I am at a loss for words."

In an effort to exacerbate the situation, the Navy had initiated the conscription of invalids out of sheer desperation. Five hundred retired soldiers, who were old, rheumatic, partially blind, missing limbs, and trembling with convulsions, arrived from the Royal Hospital in Chelsea. These soldiers, who were previously feted in parades, now marched toward ships from which they would probably never return. They were transported and hoisted onto the vessel in a state of terror and pallor. Reverend Walter, the Centurion's chaplain, stated of them, "They would in all likelihood perish unnecessarily due to lingering and painful diseases."

A significant number of individuals were unable to advance that far. A man who disappeared on a wooden limb was among the nearly half of the invalids who deserted as they limped toward Portsmouth. Walter observed that "all those who possessed the physical strength and mobility to exit Portsmouth deserted."

As the last of them were loaded onto ships, Cheap stood on the deck, his visage contorted in terror. It was no longer classified as a Military Campaign. It was a conscription of the condemned, an exodus of the broken.

Nevertheless, on August 23, 1740, Anson ordered the semaphore to be unmoored after nearly a year of stagnation. One of the Centurion's weapons was discharged by Cheap as he advanced. The harbor reverberated with the sound of a promise that had been ultimately fulfilled. Officers emerged. Boatswains whistled. Men sprinted across the decks, untying sails, extinguishing lanterns, and dragging hammocks. The five men-of-war, the reconnaissance sloop Trial, and two supply ships—the Anna and the Industry—were propelled into motion.

Eyes fixated on the sea, Cheap inhaled the salt air. Debt collectors, bureaucrats, and the acrid smoke of London were situated behind him. Purpose was anticipated. Or so it appeared.

Their departure was anything but tranquil. They were betrayed by the breezes, which abruptly changed direction. The inexperienced landsmen were terrified as the squadron collided with other ships. They made two additional attempts to depart, but the gales forced them to retreat. the London Daily Post announced on September 5 that the fleet was still "waiting for a favourable wind," as everyone had anticipated.

Afterward, the wind shifted on the evening of September 18. The horizon widened as the ships shook and the rigging was set in motion. Even the conscripts, who were disillusioned and seasick, experienced a moment of optimism while aboard the Wager. One of the men wrote in his journal, "The men were elevated with the expectation of becoming immensely wealthy." "And in a few years, they would return to Old England with the wealth of their enemies."

"Cheap stood tall on the quarterdeck, his hands firmly grasping the rail as the sea finally swallowed the coast behind them." The crimson pendant of Anson was launched from the mast of the Centurion. The cannons saluted. Smoke curled into the evening sky.

They had departed from England, but they had not left behind its lunacy. They had fled the piers, but they had not fled the decay. They had succeeded in surpassing all expectations.

The upcoming events included a storm, starvation, and devastation. A vessel was destroyed in the waters off Patagonia. The mutiny that shattered loyalty and turned men against their commanders. Eventually, a courtroom would be established, located far from the sea, where survivors would engage in a battle not only for their reputations, but also for the very narrative of truth.

_____ * * * _____

Chapter 2
A Gentleman Volunteer

Before there was a disaster, before there was mutiny, murder, or the cold metal clang of a gavel inside a naval courtroom, there was a cry in the dark.

"Rouse out, you slumbering masses!" "Rouse out!"

In the fetid blackness of the Wager's orlop deck, the ship's lowest tier below the hold, sixteen-year-old John Byron was startled to consciousness. The vile bilgewater, which was reeking of rot and despair, pooled and pulsed beneath him. He was unable to determine whether it was day or night. It was inconsequential. The light was unable to penetrate this depth. Orders were the sole exception.

Boatswain John King and his colleagues rushed through the ship like war drums, shouting and whistling through the decks, above him. Byron and the other midshipmen, who were crammed shoulder-to-shoulder in narrow hammocks stretched between beams, scrambled to dress in the dark, being cautious not to bump heads on the five-foot-high ceiling. The Wager had been at sea for only two weeks, and the wood appeared to be weeping with anguish. There was no opportunity to bathe. Absence of privacy. The ritual of survival in a location where every inch of space denoted status and every sound served as a reminder of the fragility of one's body.

Byron's family was of noble descent, with roots dating back to the Norman Conquest. He spent his boyhood beneath the spires of Newstead Abbey, the family estate that was situated adjacent to Sherwood Forest. A mother who was proud of her son and lineage inscribed his name into the glass of a monastery window. And now, he was sleeping above a pool of human runoff, his possessions crowded into a sea chest that served as a chair, desk, and surgical table in the event that the voyage became bloody.

He was not the only one. The Wager was a floating realm, with a society that was as intricate as the decks themselves. Ropes were hauled by boys as young as six, while toothless chefs in their eighties worked alongside them. Some were noble volunteers, while others were destitute conscripts who were forcibly removed from London's streets or merchant ships by press gangs. John Duck, a free Black sailor, was one of them. His presence was both remarkable and perilous, as he faced the possibility of being sold into servitude if he were captured by Spanish forces. The ship was a boiling mixture of hope, resentment, and dread, a crucible of every class and color. The Wager had collected some of its darkest fragments, and one observer referred to such a man-of-war as "an epitome of the world."

The carpenter's mate James Mitchell passed near, and even the watchful midshipman Byron, who was still green and attempting to live up to his family name, felt a chill. Mitchell did not speak extensively; however, his eyes were ablaze with a wrath that was unsuitable for the close proximity. Yes, Boatswain King was belligerent; however, his fury was structured. Mitchell's blazed ferociously, resembling dry timber that was awaiting a spark.

The Wager groaned and swayed beneath Byron as he ascended to the upper decks by rolling up his hammock. He was slapped by the salty air. He absorbed it with the same intensity as a man emerging from the depths of the ocean. The masts extended into the heavens in the form of spires, towering above him. The crew moved in a state of orchestrated pandemonium around him, rigging, shouting, scrubbing, and watching. They had embarked on a journey weeks prior, in pursuit of a wind that had evaded them for nearly a year. This wind would propel them beyond the limits of maps, around Cape Horn, and into waters devoid of comfort.

Nevertheless, this was not a well-oiled machine, despite its ritual. The voyage was in a state of disarray, even while at sea.

Back in Portsmouth, Cheap had observed over 240 men defect before they even reached the open sea. These men, including volunteers and pressed men, vanished at the first opportunity. A few individuals pretended to be unwell. Others simply dispersed. The press squad that was dispatched to locate replacements for the Wager had collapsed, as six of its members deserted. The Navy had filled the gaps with sick recruits, criminals, paupers, and even invalids who had been rescued from Chelsea's Royal Hospital. These men, who were either too elderly or too ill to serve on land, were now at the mercy of the sea. The Navy was in a state of desperation.

Leading up to the storm, the personnel were exhausted. The timber fell victim to decay prior to the arrival of the wave. The disease disseminated prior to the sails being filled.

The youngest Byron, the son of an empire and the soon-to-be grandfather of a poet, stood in the morning darkness of the South Atlantic, oblivious that he was entering a narrative that would haunt him for the rest of his life. The wooden table in his berth, where appendages would be severed and groans would reverberate, was not merely a reminder of the surgeon's work. It was a prophecy.

The Wager would be disassembled on a remote Patagonian coast in the near future. Her crew would gradually deteriorate into betrayal, malnutrition, and violence. The collapse of hierarchies would occur. Mitchell would disclose his authentic personality. The king would disappear into legend. Byron would undergo an ordeal that few have ever experienced, and his return would be irrevocably altered.

Survivors would not return home in triumph, but rather in scandal, years later. Into a court-martial. Into a conflict of narratives in which the ultimate victim was truth itself.

The wind struck John Byron's face like a hand, sharp, salted, and genuine, as he ascended the quarterdeck. The world appeared expansive and mechanical from this vantage point, which was elevated above the bilge-water gloom of the orlop where he was sleeping. Swaying masts were observed. The ropes creaked. Voices fluctuated like waves. And beneath it all, the Wager moved—not freely, but like a leviathan guided by unseen mechanisms. Each individual on board was one of those cogs.

As a midshipman, Byron was anticipated to be present in all locations and in no particular place. He delivered orders, examined the sails, and conveyed communications from officers whose faces were unreadable. However, his primary activity was to observe. Within days, it became apparent to him that this was more than a vessel; it was a society in motion, a world of strict boundaries and more acute divisions.

Standing at the apex of the structure, Captain David Kidd observed his domain from the same deck. Kidd possessed a level of influence that no monarch could match, as it was beyond the reach of courts or kings. At the risk of oblivion, a man disobeyed him, rather than of punishment. He served as a judge, executioner, father, and deity to his crew.

Lieutenant Robert Baynes attempted to command with less certainty beneath him. Despite the fact that he possessed two endorsements from previous commanders, the crew referred to him as "Beans"—whether out of mischief or disdain—and no one expressed an opinion. He possessed the demeanor of an individual who favored the concept of leadership over its application, who issued directives with a gentle touch and then observed them disintegrate into the air.

A maze of ranks and professions was present beneath Baynes, all of which were bound together by necessity. Thomas Clark, the ship's commander, supervised its instruments and tracked its course. The helmsmen grasped the great double wheel with blistered hands after the quartermaster relayed the information. Sailmakers, artisans, gunners, and surgeons were incapable of evading their obligations. The surgeon's assistants, who were referred to as "loblolly boys," acquired their title not from the practice of medicine, but rather from the porridge they distributed to patients in a fever hospital.

The mariners, too, resided by tier. The sail-handlers, who walked the rigging like spiders spun in the clouds, climbed into the heavens. Their nerves were of iron. The "forecastle men," who were seasoned and disfigured, fought the wind at the ship's prow and controlled the anchors beneath them. Secondly, there were the "waisters," who were confined to land and were tasked with the tedious tasks of scraping decks and shoveling dung. They were ridiculed by mariners and disregarded by officers. Worked alongside the poultry and pigs, they endured the ridicule of every voice that was rope-hardened above them.

And then, the marines arrived in their own unique detachment. Soldiers who are dressed in naval blue. They were intended for land assaults and order-keeping, but they were rendered useless at sea. Robert Pemberton, one of their commanders, spoke scarcely. Lieutenant Thomas Hamilton, the other individual, had already been exiled from the Centurion following a knife battle with another officer. He now stalked the Wager like a flame in a powder room. Hamilton would be the one to subdue the company if they were to rise.

The ship was transformed into a living, breathing mechanized beast in the eyes of Byron. A sailor referred to it as "a collection of human machinery," with each individual serving as a cog or lever in the machinist's scheme. Each rope is pulled by hands that have been trained in obedience rather than liberation. Each chime signifies an order. Each silence is a menace.

Nevertheless, the language terrified Byron more than the mechanics, as it revealed how the act of speaking had been transformed by the sea. A hammock served as a shelter. The "head" is a restroom. A child was transformed into a "Jack." John Byron, the son of a nobleman, was now known as Jack Tar. He began to count time not by the hour, but by chimes that were rung at half-hour intervals, calibrated by sandglass and ritual. A single chime. Two chimes. Four hours. The conclusion of one watch marked the commencement of another. The ship continued to advance, not only across oceans but also into the hearts of its crew.

He pursued Latin whenever he had the opportunity, as was customary for gentlemen. He read Milton and Ovid, and he practiced fencing. However, it was the quadrants, knots, and lines that were now of significance. He acquired the ability to gauge speed by the number of knots in a rope that slipped through his fingertips. To interpret compass coordinates and stars. To ensure that bracing and tacking are executed without error. He acquired the ability to communicate not only as a seaman, but also as an individual who was striving to endure a language that was specifically designed to reveal vulnerabilities. Shame would follow like a shadow as a result of a single error—such as pulling the incorrect "sheets" or misinterpreting an order.

Even profanity was subject to regulations.

Even violence had its own cadence.

The cat-o'-nine-tails hung as silent punctuation in the background, a sentence that awaited transgression rather than grammar. Flogging was not an uncommon occurrence. It was considered a testament to one's fortitude to endure it without shouting out. Byron discovered at an early age that each lesson at sea was multiplied by two: one in terms of skill and one in terms of suffering.

The crew surrounding him—this tumultuous brotherhood of thieves, nobles, fugitives, orphans, and dreamers—all resided in that dual universe. Among them was John Duck, a free Black sailor, whose silence concealed the fact that apprehension resulted in enslavement. Boys who were scarcely old enough to grasp a rope were among them. Old males who had outlived both land and sea. And ghosts—individuals such as James Mitchell, the carpenter's companion, whose glare chilled Byron's blood and suggested a darkness that had yet to be identified.

The Wager was not merely venturing into mysterious waters.

It was being drawn into a crucible, a place where the soul's raw shape was the only thing that remained after the identities were burned away. Byron, who was born into privilege, was now bowed by cold, cut by wind, and reshaped by the labor of obedience. And although he was unaware of it at the time, the world he was being instructed to protect would abandon him. The officers who were in charge would fragment. Those with whom he lodged would develop a feral demeanor. The Wager's order would be undermined by starvation, desperation, and betrayal, and the system that provided it would collapse.

He would endure a catastrophe.

He would endure privation.

Ultimately, he would be compelled to testify in a London courtroom as a witness to the most egregious dissolution of British command that has ever been documented at sea.

Moments such as this existed prior to the catastrophe, prior to the island, and prior to the onset of hunger and cold.

John Byron had arrived at the sea as the son of nobility, but he was gradually evolving into a different person—one who was more vigilant, more insatiable, and more in tune with the changing world. Discipline and peril were not the sole aspects of life on The Wager. The days were punctuated by periods of laughter, play, and cuisine that, despite its salted and toughness, satisfied the stomach and added color to the environment.

In his berth, Byron, Isaac Morris, and Henry Cozens ate oatmeal, peas, biscuits, and any preserved meat that was available. They were confined to a small corner of the ship during mealtimes. The food was unremarkable, but it was abundant, and the company was more inviting than the gusts of wind outside.

Seamen gathered in groups of eight on the gun deck to share meals on suspended wooden planks that were lowered from the beams. These messes were not merely dining units; they were carefully selected families—loyal, bawdy, and securely bound. They exchanged stories, taunted each other, and forged a bond based on trust in the presence of water and wind, rather than blood. They also consumed daily rations of beer or spirits. Cozens was particularly appealing to Byron, as he described him as amicable when sober—a subtle reference to the perpetual threat that existed within friendship.

The atmosphere was more optimistic on Sundays. The word was received: "All hands to play!" The warship, which was constructed as a floating fortress for combat, was abruptly converted into a temporary carnival. Clattering backgammon boards were heard. To the accompaniment of fiddles, sailors performed reels. The boys climbed the rigging in a manner reminiscent of primates at play. Commodore Anson, who was typically inscrutable and reserved, would engage in card games with a quiet ruthlessness. His gaze did not disclose anything. His expression suggested that he was contemplating his options. Nevertheless, he appreciated music, and the fiddlers' melodies caused the officers to relax, as the sails above them swayed in time with the reels and shanties.

A hymn that was frequently played was an ode to the War of Jenkins' Ear: They severed his ears and slit his nose...

They then threw his ear at him with a jeer, saying, "Take it to your master" in derision...

However, it is possible that Byron's preferred ritual occurred at the conclusion of the day, when the sun began to set and the seasoned travelers convened to recount tales of storms that were endured, lovers who were abandoned, and spirits that were observed in the mists. These narratives were imbued with an unusual form of immortality, as if recounting them aloud might mitigate mortality for an additional period.

At that time, Byron initiated his writing. With wide-eyed amazement, his journal was filled. The most unexpected was that everything was astonishing. He documented the gleam of a black-feathered bird with an eagle's crest, the creak of the masts, and the shape of the waves. The ship was not merely a vessel. It was a stage, and he was a participant in a narrative that was more significant than anything at Newstead Abbey.

Then, the summons that all midshipmen dreaded and eagerly anticipated arrived: "Aloft you go!"

It had come time to ascend.

He had practiced on the mizzenmast, which was the shortest. The mainmast, which stood nearly one hundred feet above the water, was a cathedral of rope and sway. He would perish if he were to plummet from this height, as it has done to others. Two boys fell, their skulls cracking open against the iron muzzles of the guns, and one captain gazed in despair as they fell. Byron had encountered accounts of such fatalities. He was now required to confront the mast independently.

He did not hesitate. It was one thing to be noble. What was of importance at this time was to be useful and to endure. He assured a seaman, "I am capable of withstanding adversity on an equal basis with the most adept of you." "And I must employ myself to their advantage."

He ascended on the windward side, where the heel of the ship would urge his body into the ropes, rather than away from them. A distance of ten feet. Twenty. The ratlines vibrated beneath his boots. His hands wavered as he held the shrouds. The deck was already a world that was distant from him. He faced his first significant challenge at the main yard, the horizontal spar: whether to ascend through the "lubber hole," a small, secure aperture in the platform, or to confront the futtock shrouds, the ropes that curved out like the curved spines of a ribcage.

The pit was only occupied by cowards.

The ropes were selected by Byron.

He bent his body rearward into the open sky, clinging to lines that were slick with tar, as he shinnied up. His face was buffeted by the breeze. Wood was scuffed by his boots. His extremities were on fire. And then— he was on the platform. A brief halt. Then, there is an increase.

The mast was composed of three connected pieces of timber, each of which was thinner and less forgiving than the previous one. The lines converged, narrowing to knife-edges, as he ascended. He advanced beyond the main-topmast yard, traversed the crosstrees, and ascended thereafter. Presently, each action was perilous. There were no ratlines to grasp. The mast swayed like a pendulum in a tempest, and the ropes were taut. He ascended through the air, rather than on it.

He stood, barely, at the topgallant yard, the topmost point of the mainmast. He held a single rope in his grasp, and the expanse of the sky stretched out before him. He could observe the other ships in Anson's squadron, their bows slashing through the sea and their sails stretched like wings. Beyond them, there is only water.

Byron was no longer merely the junior son of a noble family in that location. He was now known as Jack Tar. A seaman. An eyewitness. Between the infinite blue expanse above and below, a youth transforms into a man.

In that immense, wind-cut silence, he experienced what Herman Melville would later refer to as the sailor's exaltation: "a wild delirium..." a sensation of joy, excitement, and pulsation that permeates the entire system, as you are lifted into the clouds of a tempestuous sky and suspended between the heavens and the earth, resembling a judgment angel.

However, what John Byron was unable to observe was the fate that awaited them all, perched high above the quarterdeck.

Hunger.

The chill.

The event of disintegration.

Mutiny.

The scaffold.

A court.

The truth was ingrained in the bones of every ship: the performance of the others determined the fate of each individual. A solitary failure, a single malignant soul, could bring it all down.

Additionally, it would.

The lament, which was sharp, electric, and unmistakable, resounded at dawn on October 25, 1740.

"Welcome to the land!"

The lookout on the Severn was the first to observe the jagged silhouette that had materialized in the blue-black haze, as if a secret were emerging from the depths. The sun had not yet surmounted the rim of the sea. Guns were discharged in response to a signal. Flashing lanterns illuminated the area. And as John Byron rubbed the sleep from his eyes and hurried to the deck, he also caught sight of it: Madeira, dark and brooding, breaking the endless ocean horizon with the promise of relief.

The squadron, which consisted of five men-of-war, a reconnaissance sloop, and two supply vessels, had been at sea for thirty-seven days, a journey that was already three times longer than Commodore Anson expected. The wind had shifted against them. Morale had deteriorated. As they anchored in the inlet on the eastern side of the island, it was evident that the southern summer they had hoped to capitalize on in order to navigate Cape Horn without incident was ebbing away.

Reverend Walter, who was constantly the chronicler of both divine providence and practical foreboding, confessed what others were afraid to say aloud: the forthcoming passage around South America—Cape Horn in winter—was no longer theoretical. It was unavoidable. And it caused them to be horrified.

Nevertheless, Madeira had its advantages. The island, which was renowned for its perpetual spring and wine that had a flavor of sweetness and sun, provided a fleeting glimpse of paradise. Alongside wood and water, barrels of wine were carried into the holds. However, Anson maintained that this stay would be brief. There was insufficient time to relax beneath palm trees. He desired to depart before his men's doubts became entrenched.

However, it was already too late.

The initial strike was delivered on November 3. The son of the renowned Admiral John Norris, Captain Richard Norris of the Gloucester, submitted a resignation request. He attributed his body's deterioration since his departure to illness. However, it was perceived as cowardice by all, including Anson.

Anson, a man of frigid self-possession, was unable to conceal his contempt. Subsequently, he would contribute to the creation of a regulation that mandated that any individual who was found to have acted cowardly during a battle would be subject to death. Even Reverend Walter, who was himself a sickly man with a philosopher's spirit, did not feel any sympathy. He wrote, "Fye upon it!" "It is an impure passion." Norris, the individual who resigned, would subsequently be accused of retreating from a combat and subsequently disappear before his own court martial could be conducted. His name was transformed into an apparition.

The resignation caused a cascading effect throughout the chain of command.

Promotions were cumulative. The Gloucester was under the command of the commander of the Pearl. Captain Dandy Kidd, a benevolent and compassionate officer who was adored on the Wager, was transferred to the Pearl. George Murray, the son of a nobleman and the erstwhile commander of the Trial sloop, succeeded him. New regulations were implemented by him. Tensions have arisen. Additionally, there are new individuals.

Alexander Campbell now occupied the space adjacent to Byron in his already cramped midshipmen's accommodations. Campbell was a contradiction in person—he was fifteen years old, Scottish, and had a keen tongue. Despite his youth, he maintained an imperious demeanor. He rapidly adopted the demeanor of an officer-in-waiting, wielding his fists more readily than companionship, barking orders, and quoting the captain. The narrow world of Byron, who had recently begun to find solace in the camaraderie of Morris and Cozens, was now invaded.

Nevertheless, the second revelation dwarfed even this disruption.

A Spanish armada, consisting of five formidable vessels, one of which was equipped with seventy-four guns and seven hundred men, was poised off the western coast of Madeira. The governor of Madeira leisurely announced the news, as if it were the weather. Their objective is to intercept and eliminate Anson's squadron.

There was a release of information regarding the British expedition. The squadron's movements, including their purported secrecy, were confirmed by Spanish documents captured later in the conflict. Anson was not embarking on a voyage of enigma. He was inadvertently navigating into a trap.

The transition from a covert strike force to a hunted fleet commenced at this point.

Lanterns were extinguished that evening. The ships proceeded in silence. Byron stood on deck, his young hands clenched to the rail, as he observed the stars blink above and the black shape of Madeira diminish behind them. He could detect the change—not in the wind, but in his intention. The squadron was no longer a predator. It was prey.

They would now sail not only with sails, but also with shadows.

Frightened.

Recognizing that they were being observed, they were aware that Spanish gunners were poised beyond the dark line of horizon. The sea had expanded significantly, and it would no longer permit their passage with such ease.

John Byron was unable to anticipate the events that were to come. That the Wager would not endure the Pacific. That its soldiers would collide with a Patagonian littoral. They would be consumed by that appetite. Their separation would be precipitated by murder and mutiny. That, years later, a court-martial would attempt to reconstruct the truth from the fragments of their memories and minds.

Nevertheless, that evening, as the squadron vanished from Madeira's port, leaving behind wine and warmth, Byron sensed it—a small thing that was closing in. Not mortality. Not yet.

However, it is comparable.

_____ * * * _____

Chapter 3
THE GUNNER

The sound of a constant and ominous drumbeat, resembling the thud of a heartbeat, penetrated the hull. The drum's skin was struck by one of the marines on His Majesty's Ship Wager in the darkness, and the sound reverberated throughout the vessel, resembling the pulse of war. The "call to battle," the "beating to quarters," was the summons to all capable individuals on board to assume arms. Some men were half-dressed, while others were already feverish from anticipation, as they lurched from slumber or silence. The timbers were saturated with oil and seawater, and boys ran across them barefoot. Time was not allotted for compassion. The surf was impatient.

Buckets, barrels, and tools were hurled aside on the gun deck, as were any other loose items that could potentially shatter into flying shards and impale a friend or adversary in the midst of a broadside. Each individual was assigned a position; however, the order was precariously balanced on the brink of chaos. Discipline was the sole defense in the chaos of naval combat. The powder monkeys, the youngest crew members, were scrawny boys who were frequently no older than thirteen or fourteen. They ran through the pandemonium. One of them, with his legs scarcely stable, scurried toward the magazine room, the ship's heavily guarded and locked chamber of powder and death. No flame ventured to cross its threshold. No candle flickered in the vicinity of its entrance. It was a space that emanated anxiety and silence.

The youngster turned to run after retrieving a heavy cartridge, which was packed with several pounds of gunpowder, with shaky hands. The planks were struck by his boots. The charge was passed to his gunnery team as he navigated through a forest of moving bodies, dodging flailing arms and groaning rigging. The precision with which they labored was reminiscent of that of skilled and frightened men. The cannon's pharynx was obstructed by the cartridge. Subsequently, an iron ball—eighteen pounds of cast iron—was introduced, followed by wadding. The gun was subsequently propelled forward on its heavy wooden carriage until the muzzle was visible through the porthole, where it was targeted blindly into the void.

Afterward, conflagration ensued.

The command was delivered in a manner reminiscent of a spell: "Prick the cartridge..." Aim the firearm at... You may retrieve your match... "Fire!"

The matchman, a bleak individual with soot-stained hands, inserted a slow-burning wick into the touchhole of the cannon and proceeded to vault away. The gun detonated a heartbeat later. A man standing behind the cannon would have been pulverized by the monstrous force with which it recoiled. The gun deck was enveloped in smoke, resembling a thundercloud. The air was shook by the force of the impact. At a velocity exceeding 1,000 feet per second, the shot ripped through the atmosphere. Thunder rumbled on both sides of the vessel.

However, this was not a combat. It was a rehearsal.

The exercise was ordered by Commodore Anson in order to prepare his men for a nearby Spanish armada, as he became increasingly paranoid. To reside on The Wager was to inhabit a house of spirits, where each sound could be interpreted as a signal and each night as a precursor to a massacre.

One man, John Bulkeley, the ship's gunner, stood at the epicenter of the action. He did not recoil, and he moved through the smoke and fire with the precision of a figure that had already been tamed by the worst.

He was not a patrician, a commissioned officer with a powdered wig, or a father in Parliament. He was a man who had been raised from the depths of the Navy, a man who was composed of tar and tendon, blood and iron. The well born midshipmen had scoffed at Bulkeley, who had once been among the lowest of the low, cleaning bilges and hauling lines. However, he had obtained his warrant—a technical rank issued by the Navy Board, not the Crown—through his extraordinary diligence and mastery of the gunnery craft. He was now the steward of the ship's instruments of death.

He was aware of each and every projectile and cannon. He packed munitions with his teeth and mixed powder with surgeon-like precision. He was a man whose hands were covered in calluses, while others wore rings, and his breath was acrid with salt and black powder. He employed faith, fire, and lead as his instruments.

Nevertheless, Bulkeley was not solely a warrior. He was a man of God. He carried The Christian's Pattern: or, A Treatise of the Imitation of Jesus Christ in his bosom, in addition to his cartridges. He was disheartened by the fact that religious services were seldom conducted at The Wager. He expressed his dissatisfaction with the Navy's disregard for devotion and prayer in his journal. He was of the opinion that suffering drew a person closer to the divine, and he believed that this journey—this ordeal by fire and water—might bring him closer to salvation, or possibly obliteration.

He was a leader, albeit not by birthright. His uncommon distinction during the voyage was the command of a watch. This was exceedingly uncommon for a gunner. He quietly documented it in his journal with a sense of pride: "Despite my role as the ship's gunner, I was responsible for maintaining a watch throughout the entire voyage." However, these accomplishments were not accompanied by any social advancement. His midshipmen, such as young John Byron, were still of a superior class, were more appropriately attired, and were more likely to be immortalized in royal commendations and oil paintings. Bulkeley's legacy consisted solely of his ink-stained pages; he possessed no portrait.

His logbooks, which were composed on thick paper with quills that could penetrate seawater and storms, meticulously recorded every aspect of his journey, including wind, bearing, and extraordinary incidents. However, Bulkeley went one step further. Poetry, scripture, and private reflection comprised his journals. He composed not only to recollect, but also to serve as a witness.

"Bold were the men who first spread the new sails on the ocean, when the worst-case scenario was a shipwreck: We now find more dangers from man alone than from the rocks, the billows, and the wind."

He was correct. The Wager's company was not destroyed by the sea when they were eventually wrecked off the coast of Chile, scattering, starving, and turning on one another. Men were the ones in question. Mutiny was precipitated by hunger. The authority was overthrown. The sophisticated chain of command was corroded.

Bulkeley's role expanded beyond that of a gunner in the aftermath. He assumed the roles of judge, guardian, and savior for those who persisted. He debated, fought, and foraged. In response to the fear of others, he rose. He penned after the mutinous took authority.

Additionally, his writing would serve as the basis for his assessment.

A court-martial was held months later, as the surviving crew struggled to return home across oceans and continents. Officers provided testimony. Fingers were indicated by sailors. Careers were precariously poised. And Bulkeley's journal was introduced into this chamber of polished wood and powdered wigs—his meticulous records of treachery and truth, his stoic voice, and his smudged ink.

It was not merely a logbook. A reckoning was in order.

The judges reviewed accounts of commanders who had failed, of men who had abandoned their duties, and of a broken chain of command. They read of the firing of cannons and the unspoken petitions, of divine faith in the face of human cruelty. Additionally, they perceived the voice of a single individual—one who was unrefined, unyielding, and forthright.

John Bulkeley, the gunner who had no lineage but fire and ink, had not only survived the disaster of The Wager. He had survived the dissolution of authority. He had penned his truth in a world where it was frequently submerged.

In doing so, he turned the tide—not with gunpowder, but with testimony.

A thin layer of mist hung like a veil between heaven and purgatory, and the sky bled into the sea in a smear of gray on a chilled November morning. Slicing through the subdued dawn, a cry resounded from the masthead of The Wager.

"Away we go!"

The men's drowsy routines were abruptly interrupted by the sharp and urgent call. The sound was such that it caused every hair on a sailor's arm to stand on end, serving as a reminder of the perilous nature of life at sea. The squadron was promptly informed of Captain Anson's status, which was now more akin to a fable than a human. He directed his five men-of-war to form a line of battle, their dark hulls forming an immense iron necklace that stretched across the sea. It was the oldest strategy in the book: to consolidate power, establish symmetry, and prepare for war. The entire chain could collapse if a single node is compromised.

However, the sea showed little regard for the formations. Fog and wind were deceivers. Captains had long since acquired the skill of deception, as they were cognizant of the delicate balance between silence and sails. They stole wind, feigned distress, and even beckoned in foreign tongues to lure enemies near before baring their teeth in fire. The sea was not merely a battlefield; it was also a chessboard.

Captain Cheap, who had recently been appointed to command The Trial, was instructed to pursue. With a fervor that was equally motivated by ambition and obligation, he obliged. The Trial proceeded apace. John Bulkeley, located behind him, stood calmly among the gunners on The Wager. His eyes were narrowed with suspicion, and his hands were already moving instinctively toward preparation. Powder was measured and guns were cleansed. Death could result from a moment's hesitation in such a pursuit.

The shadow on the horizon was not a Spanish man-of-war, but a Dutch merchant vessel, which was peaceful and unaware. Two hours passed before the shadow was disclosed. A warning shot was discharged by Cheap. The Dutchmen yielded, making a hesitant, perplexed turn. The crisis was resolved. The males exhaled. Inaccurate alarm.

However, an even more malevolent adversary had already entered the vessel without detection.

It did not don a uniform or hoist a flag. It did not emit cannon fire or issue threats. It silently crept beneath collars and nestled in seams. The fleet had transformed into a floating hive of illness, as it was cramped and perspired in its own salt and breath.

Typhus.

The siege commenced without any prior notification. Initially, the junior. The lads who had previously adeptly scaled the rigging were now unable to rise from their hammocks. Afterward, the pressed men, many of whom were already ill before they arrived on deck, collapsed in a state of fever, trembling, and being drenched in their own vomit. A few individuals wept. Some individuals spoke incoherently, grasping at the wood or attempting to throw themselves overboard in search of solace in the sea. Bulkeley observed them in horror, feeling helpless. There was no defense, except for prayer, and even that appeared inadequate.

Henry Ettrick, the ship's surgeon, made every effort to assist. He converted a lower deck into a temporary sickbay by suspending hammocks in areas where sunlight was scarce. The phrase "under the weather" was brought to life in this darkness, as men were protected from the wind and rain but were ensnared in a pestilent cloud of perspiration, bile, and death. Ettrick was not unfamiliar with brutality. He was capable of cutting off a limb in a matter of minutes. A machine, consisting of fifteen pounds of wood and gears, was even constructed by him to repair fractured quadriceps. However, what about this? This was distinct. The pestilence could not be eradicated by any blade.

Bacteria were unknown to them. More than a century would pass before germ theory was established. The men were of the opinion that the illness was caused by the devil's breath, moisture, or foul odors present in moldy sails or unwashed meat. They searched for an invisible poison by sniffing bilges and containers. A sailor once remarked, "A man dared not open his mouth lest he choke on the bugs." The air was infested with an abundance of insects.

The fleet commenced to deteriorate.

Even so, Bulkeley persevered. He turned his attention inward. He believed that God was in the process of testing him. He reread The Christian's Pattern under the lantern's light and buried his face in prayer as others laid to rest their loved ones. The officers convened in secret on other vessels. In an effort to invigorate the decks below, the carpenters were instructed to create six new openings in the hull of each man-of-war to allow air to penetrate just above the waterline.

It was inadequate.

The surgeons, who were inundated with work, continued to work until they collapsed. Tobias Smollett, a former naval surgeon's mate and future novelist, would one day write of such scenes: "I was much less surprised that people should die on board than that any sick person should recover." He was not mistaken.

The toll struck once more on The Wager.

The bell tolled softly. A corpse was removed from the sick ward, with a cannonball sewn to the feet and wrapped in a stiffened hammock. The nostril was punctured by a final stitch, marking the final, bleak test of life. He remained motionless.

Swiftly, the funeral was conducted. The crew convened in a state of solemnity. The burial prayer was read aloud by Captain Murray, who was pensive and pale. The prayer stated, "We therefore commit his body to the deep." The Union Jack was eliminated. The bar was elevated. The cadaver disappeared in a single splash beneath the gray surface as it silently slid into the water. His sea cache would be auctioned. His name would be murmured, and then it would dissipate.

Bulkeley observed the scene, his expression frozen, his spirit battered but unbroken. He was surrounded by individuals with whom he had previously trained, slept, and shared laughter. Now they were mere shadows, dissolving into the depths.

However, none of this—not the pestilence nor the false alarms—would be able to match the impending disaster.

The deceased would cease to be silent in the cold, formal stillness of a naval courtroom months later. Their destinies would be proclaimed through testimony and logbooks, through smudged ink and cold recollections. Bulkeley's personal journal—detailed, meticulous, and damning—would be submitted as evidence. It was not merely a record. That ledger was a record of judgment.

The Wager's narrative would be recounted in the presence of polished shoes and powdered hairstyles, as well as the scent of salt memory and polished wood. A narrative that encompasses not only survival but also insurrection, moral collapse, the abandonment of one's code in pursuit of life, and a truth that not all officers were willing to confront.

And the Navy would tremble when that truth was revealed, when Bulkeley's words reverberated through the corridors, for The Wager had not merely been lost to the sea.

It had been destroyed by humans.

In the midst of the whispering murmurs of the wind and the creaking hulls of empire's ambition on November 16, 1740, two merchant ships—The Anna and The Industry—indicated to Commodore Anson that their service was complete. They asserted that they had fulfilled their contract with the Royal Navy and were now eager to return to England. But it was not obligation that motivated them to pursue a departure. It was terror. Typhus, an invisible predator, had established its lair in the fleet's holds, and every individual who was still breathing feared that he might be the next to succumb.

Cape Horn appeared to the south as the southernmost point of the Earth. The worst was yet to occur.

Anson, who was fatigued but calculating, considered the repercussions. However, the squadron was unable to accommodate the cargo of both store ships, despite the fact that the quantities of brandy, salt pork, and canvas they carried were essential. Ultimately, he discharged only The Industry, the more dilapidated of the two vessels. In addition to surplus provisions, she would transport something considerably more valuable: letters.

This would be the first and potentially final opportunity for many members of the squadron to communicate with their loved ones back home. The officers were compelled to compose an urgent message. Midshipmen, mariners, surgeons, and even marines scribbled notes by candlelight, occasionally in tears. The ship's gunner, John Bulkeley, capitalized on this fleeting thread to the shore and dispatched a letter to his wife in Portsmouth. He informed her, with the composure of an individual who had witnessed too many deaths, that he was still alive, albeit ailing. That the fever, regardless of its origin, had not yet claimed him. It is possible that God had spared him for a cause.

He folded the letter with calloused fingertips, unaware that it would never reach her. Unaware that the Spanish would occupy The Industry shortly after they departed. This would result in the words intended to comfort a distant family dissolving into a foreign sea.

The final containers were lifted from The Industry three days later. Bulkeley's log entry was sparse: The Industry store-ship parted ways. A mere ten syllables. A slow tide of melancholy gathered behind them.

Death was no longer a threat or rumor by December. It was consistent. Reverend Walter, pallid and shook, documented that more than sixty-five individuals had been compelled to enter the sea. He asserted that the illness did not only result in death, but also persisted. Even the ones that were recovered were mere shells, and they were trailing their hollowed frames across the decks. The most experienced specialist in the squadron, the chief surgeon, passed away on December 10. No one else possessed the necessary knowledge to succeed him.

Nevertheless, the vessels continued to advance southward. Bulkeley monitored the water on a daily basis. It was the sole constant—and yet, he observed, it was a tapestry of emotions. It shone like glass on certain days and thrashed like judgment on others. He wrote that it once turned crimson, resembling blood, as if nature itself was involved in the killing.

But on December 17, a change occurred: land. The outline of St. Catherine's Island, which is situated off the coast of Brazil, was defined by a smudge on the horizon. Anson issued the directive to port. They required recuperation. They required a foundation of earth beneath their feet.

St. Catherine was not a sanctuary. It was once the residence of the Guaraní people; however, disease and colonization had devastated it. Outlaws, who had escaped justice in other regions of Brazil, had now taken control of the area, creating a lawless haven in the underbrush. However, it sufficed as salvation for Anson's fleet.

The ill were transported to the shore. Old sails were utilized to construct tents, and flames were ignited. With others, Bulkeley and Byron traveled inland to hunt wild boars, monkeys, and even toucans—bright-feathered omens of a world untroubled by conflict. The location was referred to as "a druggist's shop" by Lieutenant Saumarez due to the abundance of medicinal plants. Nevertheless, mortality ensued. The island was the site of the deaths of eighty men, who were interred in shallow graves without any markers. Their memory was formed from sand, not stone.

Christmas arrived and dissipated like a mist. The day itself resulted in the deaths of three individuals. The only sounds were the dull thud of repairs, the sound of coughing, and the sound of wooden masts being repaired, sails being patched, and barrels being scrubbed with vinegar. There were no carols or candlelit prayers. The cockroaches and rodents that scurried through every crevice were extinguished by smoking charcoal fires. The fleet was preparing for the passage to Cape Horn. However, its essence was already tattered.

They departed on January 18, 1741. Into cyclones.

The initial event was swift and unkind. The mast of the Trial sloop cracked like a dry twig while eight topmen were aloft. Broken and bloodied, seven were recovered. One was drowned after being strangled by the rigging that he had previously danced across, much like a spider in the breeze.

And then, the Pearl vanished.

Bulkeley's heart clenched as he unsuccessfully surveyed the horizon. A day has elapsed. Afterward, there are two. Then, a week. They were apprehensive about her disappearance. However, on February 17, a sentry yelled, "Sail!" The Pearl was the name. However, The Pearl diverted when Anson directed the Gloucester to approach.

She was in motion.

For what reason?

The response was delivered in fragments, delivered in a hushed tone by her surviving officers. It was discovered that the Pearl had encountered Spanish warships. The armada of Pizarro. Five of them. A red pendant, which was nearly interchangeable with Anson's, was launched by one of the individuals. The Pearl approached them, believing them to be allies. They discovered the deception too late.

The Spanish pursued them at a rate of five to one. The Pearl had discarded its own longboat, oars, and containers in order to escape. The personnel prepared for the impact. The sea in front of us became inky. A reef? A deadly trap? False. Strictly animals that reproduce. Overhead, the vessel glided. The Spanish hesitated. "And the Pearl vanished into the night."

However, the pursuit had resulted in substantial losses. Supplies were misplaced. Lives in a similar manner. Furthermore, the most distressing development was the death of Captain Dandy Kidd.

Officers recounted the final days as Bulkeley, who had served with Kidd aboard The Wager, listened. He had also succumbed to fever. Kidd had praised his crew just before the conclusion, referring to them as "brave fellows." He reconciled himself with God. He implored for an individual to supervise his son. He penned a will. He then murmured a prophecy.

A whisper that would reverberate throughout the duration of the voyage and, in due course, torment the courtroom:

"The conclusion of this expedition will be one of poverty, vermin, famine, death, and destruction."

The repercussions of that prophecy were felt throughout the organization.

Another transfer in command occurred. Murray was promoted to The Pearl. David Cheap, an individual who had not previously served as a commander, would assume responsibility for the Wager. The crew murmured beneath hammocks and behind sails. Cheap would he be impartial, or would he govern through brutality?

As is customary, Bulkeley had little to say. He recorded the modification in his journal without providing any commentary. Nevertheless, there was a stirring within the text. Suspicion. A cautionary tale.

Cape Horn had not yet been reached by the expedition. And it had already been characterized by deception, disease, and mortality. The letters had been misplaced. The petitions went unanswered. In the midst of the pandemonium, men would make decisions that would permanently fracture them, resulting in a reckoning and not just a shipwreck.

Not situated on the ocean. However, in court.

The location where names would be uttered.

And the prophecy of a single individual would be fulfilled—not as a murmur, but as a verdict.

------- * * * -------

Part Two
Into the Storm

Chapter 4
DEAD RECKONING

The deck erupted in ceremony when David Cheap entered His Majesty's Ship Wager. The saline air was filled with the shriek of boatswain's whistles. Men respectfully doffed their tarred hats in unison. The officers waited for him with the unwavering determination of men who have been taught to conceal their curiosity with grace, their hands behind their backs and their gaze riveted. But something less stable—doubt—pulsed beneath that strict formality.

Cheap had been a familiar figure, a fellow officer to the majority of the crew. Now that he was wearing the full weight of captaincy, he changed completely, becoming a symbol of total power and imperial will. In an instant, the dynamic had changed. He was no longer one of them, but suddenly he was above them, in charge of all the people on board. His austere and severe countenance showed little, but his eyes darted from one to man, lingering for a minute on youthful Midshipman Byron, who exuded admiration and ambition in equal measure, and on Gunner John Bulkeley, whose hard forehead and vigilant stillness screamed of discipline and peril.

Cheap had dreamed of this moment through slow ports and cold watches, and had waited years for it. Nevertheless, he appeared to be plagued by the same concern that had previously plagued a character in Conrad's The Secret Sharer: Would he be true to the personal ideal he had long cherished for himself now that he was here? Or would he be remade by the storm?

No time for contemplation. Being captain was a responsibility that only he could handle; it was not a philosophy.

Cheap rapidly became accustomed to the great cabin, which is the customary seat of a captain's command, with the assistance of his steward, Peter Plastow. It was bigger than any room he had ever seen on a ship, with windows looking out to sea, a wide desk, and brass accent.

He kept his most valuable item there: the letter from Commodore Anson designating him as The Wager's master. One sheet of power and ink.

He called for the crew. The quarterdeck was crowded with seasoned sailors, their features wrinkled from hunger and wind. Cheap lifted the Articles of War and commenced to recite all thirty-six rules of conduct onboard a man-of-war in a tone as measured as it was determined. There wouldn't be any intoxication. Don't steal. No blasphemy. Then, with slow, deliberate weight, he recited Article 19:

"On pain of death, no member of the fleet may speak in a seditionist or mutinous manner."

Then there was silence. Like the edge of a drawn blade, he allowed the words to linger in the sea breeze.

He was aware of what was coming.

Cape Horn, the ship graveyard at the world's tip, was the Wager's destination. It was a place where hubris was punished by nature, and it was a place of horror spoken in sailors' prayers. Unhindered by land and unabated by harbors, the oceans that surrounded the Horn surged freely around the world, gaining terrible pace as they did so. These were the waters of myth, the conveyor belts of Poseidon himself, bringing gusts that screamed like the condemned and waves that could reach the top of a cathedral.

The Wager would get through this misery.

The small funnel where the Pacific and Atlantic met with unimaginable fury was known as the Drake Passage, and it was named for survival rather than safety. Only here on Earth did a single current run all the way around the world, and it did so furiously. More than 600 times the Amazon's power, or more than four billion cubic feet of water every second, blasted across that passage. There, too, the seafloor rose, squeezing waves into hideous towers as it suddenly heaved from thirteen hundred feet to just three hundred.

Then the wind came along.

The latitudes that led to the Horn had been named by sailors almost out of dread. The Screaming Sixties followed the Furious Fifties and the Roaring Forties. These weren't analogies. They were cautions. Hurricanes were not uncommon. They were anticipated.

The men aboard The Wager muttered names for this location. The awful. The Road of Dead Men. The Hatred of the Blind Horn. A century later, Melville would refer to it as the diluted version of Dante's Inferno.

And inexpensive? He didn't recoil.

He gave the order to have the sails tested, the rigging inspected, and the provisions recounted. He didn't drink. He was serious. He drilled his crew after studying them. The men started to sense a coldness in him, even though he seldom ever raised his voice. Something more hazardous than the frost of inexperience. Definitely. Not the kind that bends when it has to.

The ocean didn't wait.

Many of the men started to recall Captain Kidd's last prophecy as The Wager got ready for the journey—a whisper that was silently passed from hammock to hammock and from mess to mast.

Kidd had declared on his deathbed that it would end "in poverty, vermin, famine, death, and destruction."

Nobody chuckled. Nobody made fun of the deceased.

Cheap had only been in command for a few weeks. The winds were not yet at their strongest. There was still the Horn to come. However, under the surface, beneath the dread, beneath the rituals, beneath the reverence, another force was stirring among the crew. An unseen force. Definitely.

Would Cheap's leadership be able to withstand the impending events?

Or would the man who was so adamantly in favor of Article 19 be the one who started the mutiny that he was trying to stop?

Bulkeley's pen would speak louder than any pistol in the hushed, wood-paneled chambers of a naval court-martial, where the answer would eventually be disclosed after being sealed in splintered lumber and buried bodies.

Where merciless and unforgettable facts that had formerly been whispered between waves would finally come to the surface.

In his cabin aboard The Wager, David Cheap stood stooped over the chart table, his brow wrinkled in the flickering lantern light. The watery maze of the Southern Ocean stretched out in front of him like a map of a battlefield. He was chilled just by the names: Desolation Island. The Famine Port. Deceit is a powerful force. The Bay of Friends' Severing. This was a cemetery with titles, not a shoreline.

The arcs of imagined lines made by men who had never ventured to sail these latitudes were etched into old paper and traced by his fingers. Latitude and longitude. The net of the cartographers. However, it provided little more than illusion here, in this region of the earth. Like many captains before him, Cheap was sailing with some degree of blindness.

He could handle latitude. At night, when their set arcs were a boon to every man who dared to look up, the stars whispered it to him. However, longitude—longitude was a conundrum that had eluded the most brilliant brains of the day. Magellan's pilots had not even mentioned it. Galileo had looked to the sky for an answer. The titan of reason, Isaac Newton, wrote, "Such a watch hath not yet been made," acknowledging his defeat.

Cheap had attempted to outdo the situation. He had a gold pocket watch with him, which is a sign of authority, vanity, and accuracy. Even during storms, he kept it close, but he was aware of its limitations. Time was unreliable at sea, as temperatures dropped and gravity changed. Dozens of miles were miscalculated due to a few minutes' inaccuracy. Before anyone could hear the splintering timber, a reef may emerge from the fog and capture a ship.

Just off their own coast, four British warships had sunk in that manner in 1707. In a split second, thirteen hundred soldiers lost. Whether it was home land or not didn't matter to the sea.

Cheap was forced to rely on dead reckoning, which is a combination of prayer, instinct, and guesswork used by sailors. He used knotted rope lines and sandglasses to measure their course and speed, correcting for wind and current. The practice was as old as sailing itself. History also demonstrated that it frequently left commanders with dead men to contend with.

But he clung to hope. February was the month. March was coming. The austral summer's lingering warmth was promised by the calendar, which undoubtedly indicated calmer waters.

However, the calendar was deceiving.

The worst period to go around Cape Horn from east to west turned out to be March. The sun would be in an equinoctial position in the southern hemisphere, straight over the equator, which exacerbated the westerlies. With fresh rage, the wind shouted. Already terrible, the waves took on a primordial quality. These latitudes—the Screaming Sixties, the Furious Fifties, and the Roaring Forties—were not given their names lightly by sailors. The sea was not an element here. It was an enemy.

The Drake Passage, the harsh gulf that separates Antarctica and South America, was in front of them. There, the sea, unrestrained by land, swung around the planet in unrestrained fury. For thirteen thousand kilometers, the waves roared, rolled, and built. They reared into giants after striking the narrowing strait. And shallows beneath them. The waves slammed aloft as the bottom abruptly elevated. Like slumbering monsters, icebergs floated. 200 mph gusts of wind were recorded.

The Horn was unmastered by any man. Not Anson. Not inexpensive. Not God.

Cheap kept the squadron close to his people. With sails reefed and artillery ready in case the Spanish arrived on the horizon, they headed south along the Argentine coast. The weather became erratic. "Uncertain boisterous weather, with so much wind and sea as made us ride very hard," observed schoolmaster Thomas.

The Trial then broke her mast. At St. Julian, a desolate harbor where the Atlantic Ocean meets the world's edge, the squadron stopped. Although it appeared abandoned presently, it was haunted by the spirits of earlier explorers. The "hogs in armor," or armadillos, darted through the underbrush. Men, however, recalled what had transpired here.

It was here where Magellan had anchored in 1520. He used blood rather than words to settle unrest that grew throughout his fleet. The remains of one mutineer were left hanging for everyone to see after he was decapitated and quartered on a nearby island.

Francis Drake came fifty-eight years later. He accused Thomas Doughty, his companion, of treason. Doughty requested an English trial. "Neither care I for the laws," Drake sneered. Drake gave the command to decapitate Doughty at the same spot where Magellan had lost blood. The decapitated head was held up by his men. "Hey! "Traitors will no longer exist," Drake said.

These tales were no longer merely folklore. They were memories. And when the Trial's mast was eventually rebuilt on February 27, 1741, an officer gestured toward the exact island where the executions had taken place. It is "the seat of infernal spirits," according to Lieutenant Saumarez.

Drake had referred to it as the Island of Judgment and True Justice.

To be more truthful, the sailors dubbed it The Island of Blood.

Cheap knew the past, yet he remained silent. He kept the Articles of War in the pocket of his coat. Article 19, which states that "no one shall utter any words of sedition or mutiny... upon pain of death," was already read out by him.

However, ink is not obeyed by the waters. And occasionally, neither do men.

St. Julian was left behind by the squadron. The temperature dropped. With an edge sharpened by prophecy and weariness, Cheap returned to command. He was aware of the risks. So did Bulkeley, who kept a journal under his cot and watched in silence from the gun deck, recording every command and every slip-up. Byron, the enthusiastic young midshipman, felt something approaching and opened his eyes wide.

And there was.

Not the Horn alone. not only the storm. But a reckoning.

No man knew—only months later, in a court lighted by oil lamps and judgment—that the unraveling had started at this precise time, at this calendar turn, at this headlong tumble downhill.

Not when the ship shattered.

No, not when the mast broke.

Now, however. when fate, chart, and command started to diverge.

Cheap led The Wager into the roaring darkness with only a broken watch and unwavering confidence.

The exhausted ships were pulled past the final coordinates of the known globe by the currents, which pulled them southward like unseen hands. The wind became into a blade—cold, harsh, ruthless—and the sea darkened to a slate-colored abyss. Snow landed on the boards like ash after drifting from the dismal sky. Men spit into their sleeves to cough. In the pause between commands, teeth chattered.

Wearing a self-made captain's uniform, Captain David Cheap stood barefoot on the quarterdeck, more dignity than warmth. His eyes were constantly looking over the horizon as his gloved hands gripped a spyglass. He didn't talk much. Authority's mouth was as tightly shut as his cabin door's latches.

The ocean was teeming with weird species all around them. Penguins, described by Purser Millechamp as half fish and half fowl, congregated in close-knit colonies on rocky outcrops, waddling in a group like inebriated drunks. With spouts that resembled cannons, great southern whales heaved from the depths. At one point, a humpback surfaced so close to the Wager that it soaked Byron's coat with seawater that was blown onto the quarterdeck. The impressionable midshipman wrote, "The sheer number of whales here is astounding." "We came extremely close to hitting one... They are the biggest sort that we have ever seen.

The sea lions were even more dangerous. Byron, his voice still tinged with incredulity, described a close encounter. He wrote, "I was attacked by one when I least expected it." "They are enormous creatures that roar horribly when enraged." He almost made it out alive.

Despite this, the ships continued to hug the South American shore. With their snow-crowned peaks slicing into the sky, the ragged Andes rose like gods in stone. Some of them flew beyond twenty thousand feet, their ancient silence unaffected by the wooden ships that scuttled underneath them.

The mist followed.

A breath from some phantom mouth swept across the sea in a strange, shifting fog. It shrouded the fleet in doubt, as though the natural rules of the earth had stopped. Millechamp noted, "It gave everything a pleasing dreadful effect." Mountains flattened after twisting into monstrous shapes. Sometimes they were castles, sometimes they were broken timbers, and sometimes they were hideous shadows at sea.

"It appeared that we were surrounded by enchantments," Millechamp said.

And it was the cruelest form of magic. A place that betrayed eyesight. A realm where reality curved through glass like light. Somewhere before crazy and beyond reason.

The twisting artery that could have sent them west, the Strait of Magellan, loomed behind them, rejected as they pressed farther into the unknown. Anson had rejected it as being too limited, too dangerous, and too uncertain. Rather, they chose the outside passage, passing by locations with sinister names like the Cape of the Holy Ghost and the Cape of Eleven Thousand Virgins. Every name muttered a caution. Every name seemed like a lost sailor's final prayer.

Behind them, the continent disappeared.

Now they had been unmoored.

A single mass, a huge island with snowy peaks and a deathly silence, loomed to the west. Tierra del Fuego. "The Land of Fire"

The embers had vanished. Just ice. When Schoolmaster Thomas looked across the slopes, he saw no color or life. He remarked, "There was not a single happy green in the entire gloomy scene." As though God had left this location in the early days of creation, there was just rock and ice.

Nevertheless, the misconceptions persisted even here.

Giants that were so tall that a man's head just reached his waist were described by Magellan's chroniclers as wandering these bottomlands. The area was dubbed Patagonia. The word itself was made up out of fear and astonishment. Pata, which means "paw" in Spanish, is supposed to have originated from the inhabitants' massive feet. Some said it was lifted from a medieval monster known as The Great Patagon.

Conquest, not amazement, was the aim of these tales. Europeans exonerated themselves by portraying the indigenous people as mythical creatures that were half monster and half human. They made it easy to smash them by turning them into giants. They told themselves that to dominate was to civilize. to conquer.

Thus, Cheap and his crew were cursed with the same titles that had formerly awed explorers.

They were more than just landscape: the snow, the whales, the fog illusions, the spectral echoes of empire. They were indicators.

Cape Horn was waiting. Storms, shipwrecks, famine, treachery, and the gradual loss of authority all played a part.

The true crash had started long before Bulkeley picked up his pen and the court-martial convened in silence, long before The Wager shattered against the rocks.

The mist was where everything started.

In the magic.

When men set sail into the desert of their own emotions, beyond the boundaries of charts.

The squadron was hovering just off the eastern claw of Tierra del Fuego, the final ledge of the known world before the vast unknown of the Pacific, by the dark night of March 6, 1741. The time had come for David Cheap and his team. the real seamanship test. Ahead was Cape Horn, a specter encased in myth and wind. And they would welcome it by command rather than by default.

They had been ordered to wait by Commodore Anson. Let the light shine. Let the men see what they were sailing into, if nothing else.

With her bow held against the wind like a beast defying a leash, the Wager floated close to the other ships. Keeping pace with the slow, ominous beat of the sea's own metronome, she rocked on the current, taut rather than tossed. The shrouds and stays shook like the rigging of a theater before tragedy, and the sky above them was black and endless.

Cheap didn't blink. He gave the order for the silent preparations. New canvas was used in place of worn sails. Every loose object was tied down, every cannon was secured. In a storm, a stray barrel may be just as lethal as a broadside. Every half hour, the bells rung. Few men slept below deck. They gazed at nothing while polishing their blades.

Even though Anson detested paperwork, he had written Cheap and the other captains comprehensive instructions that they were to learn by heart and burn in the event that the enemy closed in. The most important of these is to keep the squadron intact. He cautioned that "you will answer the contrary at your utmost peril" if you split up. The ships were supposed to wait fifty-six days and reassemble on the opposite side of the continent if they split up. They were to presume Anson was dead after that. The mission must go on even if they are not present.

Anson fired the Centurion's guns at dawn. The call was placed. With sails raised into the new morning light, the armada rushed on. The day was brisk, clear, and surprisingly so. With their lookouts positioned high and searching for "islands of ice," The Trial and The Pearl gained the lead. Slower, heavier, and more susceptible, the Anna and the Wager trailed behind.

They arrived in the Strait of Le Maire, a narrow slit between Tierra del Fuego and the jagged-toothed Isla de los Estados, or Staten Island, by ten in the morning. This served as Cape Horn's entrance.

Like a broken cathedral, the Staten Island cliffs towered over them. It was more "wild and horrorous" than even the bleak Tierra del Fuego, according to Reverend Walter. Carved by lightning and fractured by earthquakes, mountains clashed upward in sharp pinnacles. Unnerved, Millechamp gazed and described it as "a proper nursery for desperation." "The border of some other world… the diamond watch-towers along heaven's furthest frontier," Melville would later write.

White-bellied albatrosses circled overhead as they went under this stone castle. Their wings were absurdly large, eleven feet long. Near these waters, a British sailor had once killed one. Shortly thereafter, the ship went down. Coleridge transformed the story into verse, writing, "The Albatross About my neck was hung in place of the cross."

The omen was ignored. Using a hook baited in pork, Anson's men captured one and consumed it for supper.

However, it appeared that no curse could apply to this day—this stunning, dazzling morning. The sky was clear. The breeze was favorable. Through placid waters, the Centurion's lion figurehead slashed forward. The war-hardened The morning was "more pleasing than any we had seen since England," according to Reverend Walter.

The members of Cheap's team chatted, laughed, and dared to dream. Treasure was close. Kidd's final predictions of disaster—poverty, starvation, vermin, death, and destruction—were derided, even pitying.

Then the light went out.

Suddenly the sky grew gloomy. Like a trumpet of judgment, the wind howled. Massive and abrupt waves smashed against hulls like war drums as they exploded from all directions. Its gallant red lion, the Centurion's prow, dived deep before rising once more and gasping for air. Sails broke. Ropes squirmed. Masts let out a moan. The sea had decided against it.

The fleet made an effort to rally. With their noses intact but battered, most ships clawed westward. Not The Wager, though.

She moved too slowly. Too heavy. She started to drift, powerless and haunted, toward the sharp fangs of Staten Island, loaded with provisions and bad luck. The wind pushed. The current drew back. The sea seemed to have made a decision. Its offering was the Wager.

Cheap remained calm. He yelled at each man to report to his post.

With their teeth clinched against the precipitation and the wind that robbed them of their breath, topmen ascended the rigging. The rain hit them like a bullet. To breathe, they had to turn their heads. People cried out of anger, some out of pain. Soaked in chilling spray, Cheap stood motionless on the quarterdeck, giving instructions like shots.

He ordered the mains reefed and the upper sails furled. He required equilibrium. Not enough wind to roll the ship, but enough to guide them free. Every man performed his part around him. Lieutenant Baynes displayed uncommon strength. Ever the iron nerve, Bulkeley took the helm with accuracy. Young and fearless, Byron joined his pal Cozens on the rigging. John King, a frequently mutinous boatswain, kept his crew steadfast. In the middle of the surge, Cummins, his friend, and the carpenter fixed leaks. With raw hands and desperate hearts, even the awkward waisters—who were typically mocked—pulled ropes.

They were battered by wave after wave, and each time the Wager threatened to break free, the current pulled her back. The shimmering, wet, hungry rocks loomed. All of them would perish screaming from a single impact.

Cheap remained steadfast.

The island seems to have been constructed with the sole intent of "crushing the lives of fragile mortals," according to a later account by a seaman. Cheap, however, would not be defeated. He called forth all of the ship's might. And the Wager, unbelievably slowly, started to move away from the rocks.

She didn't break. She lived.

Medals were absent. No cheers. A quiet, holy pride, however, spread among the males. They had done the unthinkable. "We were very near being wrecked upon the rocks," Byron would later recollect, and "we endeavoured all in our power to make up our lost way."

Bulkeley, who is frequently disdainful, acknowledged that Cheap had displayed "personal bravery" and referred to him as "an excellent seaman."

Cheap had changed into the man he'd always wanted to be in that one instant, frozen and fierce.

A ship's master.

The storm's lord.

A captain by proof, not by commission.

The team would never see him like that again.

Because the wreck was ahead.

Then came the rebellion.

And the truth, at last, in the antiseptic, still air of a courtroom.

What started off as triumph will turn into treachery.

Additionally, Cheap, who had persevered through the storm, would have to face a trial that was far more cruel than the sea.

------- * * * -------

Chapter 5
THE STORM WITHIN THE STORM

By the second week of March 1741, the storms had stopped coming and going and had just stayed. Waves smashing like crumbling towers, wind roaring like war trumpets, and gale after gale. The sea offered no respite. The sea below was a tangle of shifting blackness, and the skies above The Wager were pitch-black.

As wave after wave crashed over the deck, throwing the 123-foot ship like a toy, John Byron, a little youngster, stood soaked to the bone, watching in wonder and fear. The Wager, which took pride in her creation, was reduced to a pathetic lifeboat in the midst of nature's wrath. Water permeated all of the joints, the planking, the seams, and even the wood's natural grain. Officers and personnel were forced to leave their accommodations when it swamped the lower decks, drowning the hammocks. The weather was present everywhere and there was no longer any location "under the weather."

Sheets of rain fell, occasionally with enough force to cause bruises. The wave pounded itself down like hammers and rose like walls. Ropes, ladders, yards, sails, and even the wheel were all saturated when the crew touched them. Hours of grasping wet rigging left their fingers scorched and burnt. The clothes never dry. The skin started to get infected.

With his legs spread wide, his feet braced like a gaucho on a charging horse, and his hands gripping anything that may keep him upright, Byron attempted to maintain his station during watch. He would be flung into the sea if he let off, even for a second. The world became even darker as lightning slashed the sky, bright enough to freeze a moment in clarity before disappearing. He didn't understand time. The night engulfed the days. In wind and water, hours bled together.

The temperature dropped. Sleet replaced the rain. Next, snow. Ice strengthened the ropes. The rigging solidified. People suffered frostbite. There is no rule below forty degrees, according to an old proverb that one sailor muttered. The temperature below fifty degrees is devoid of God. Even prayer seemed to be drowned out in the Furious Fifties.

The wind never stopped screaming and punishing. It was angry, yet it lacked rhythm. It blew "with such violence that nothing can withstand it, and the sea runs so high that it works and tears a ship to pieces," according to Byron's subsequent writing. "The most disagreeable sailing in the world," he said.

However, there were other predators than the weather.

Byron noticed his shipmates withering shortly after The Wager crossed the Strait of Le Maire. From something quieter, not from wounds. Something unfamiliar.

They ceased to get out of their hammocks. Their limbs grew hideously. Reverend Walter described the purple and black skin as "a luxuriance of fungous flesh." Unable to move or talk, men whimpered at the contact of air. As though they were being eaten alive from the inside out, a peculiar corrosion slowly made its way up their bodies, from the toes to the thighs to the shoulders.

Thomas, the schoolmaster, initially had a searing pain in his left toe. Until it spread, he didn't give it any thought. Under his skin, nodes grew. Ulcers appeared. He described "so severe joint pains...as I believed, prior to experiencing them, that human nature could never have supported."

The condition was caught by Byron himself. He would describe the agony as "the most violent imaginable."

Some guys became grotesque as the sickness spread to their faces. Their eyes bulged and turned red. They lost their teeth in clusters. Their hair did the same. They had a rotten breath odor. It was "the scent of the grave, before you enter it," according to one sailor.

The substance that held their bones together, cartilage, appeared to melt. Old scars came back. One man saw his old scars rip and flow again after being hurt decades ago at the Battle of the Boyne. The impossible was seen by Reverend Walter: a long-healed bone that "dissolved again, as if it had never been consolidated."

Then the crazy struck.

The sailors started having hallucinations. They talked of rivers, animals, music, verdant pastures, and wives they had long since forgotten. Then they fell into despair in the following breath. Reverend Walter described it as "a strange dejection of the spirits." It was accompanied by "the most dreadful terrors, shiverings, and tremblings." It was compared as "the falling down of the whole soul" by one medical specialist.

A few men went completely crazy.

The Wager had ventured into the world of scurvy as well as the Furious Fifties.

The sea's huge pestilence.

They had no idea what had caused it. The cold was blamed by some. The meat was accused by some. Some claimed it was God's wrath. But it was indiscriminate, whatever it was. It hit both cabin boys and officers. More seamen had been killed by it than by gunshot, drowning, and all other illnesses put together. It suddenly swept through the ranks of Anson's ships like a creeping fire.

The cook was unable to start his stove either. There was no possibility of flame since the storm was too strong. As a result, the men shivered, gnawed at slabs of raw salted meat in the dark, and their mouths were bleeding from ulcers.

To take his next watch one night, Byron stumbled through the ship's soggy labyrinth. They soaked the lamps. There was silence on the lower decks. Looking around, he stepped out into the quarterdeck's blast of wind.

Almost no guys remained to keep guard.

He remarked, "The greatest part had been disabled through sickness and exhaustion."

After the chief surgeon passed away, Henry Ettrick, a surgeon, relocated to the Centurion and conducted frantic autopsy. He opened corpses on the orlop deck while wearing a dirty smock. Like rot, their flesh peeled away. He claimed that their bones became "quite black." Thick and heavy, "like black and yellow liquor," their blood poured out.

Ettrick attributed it to the cold. He could only accept the reality, though, when he was informed that scurvy also plagued ships in the tropics; the cause might be kept a "whole secret."

Nobody was aware of their cause of death.

All they knew was that it couldn't be stopped.

The hull was pummeled by the storms. The ropes went cold. The planks were scratched by the waves. Men cried silently. laughed without cause. In their hammocks, they perished.

And Cape Horn waited far ahead, there in the unseen darkness.

And then—damn it.

Then there was mutiny.

And then—a London courtroom, where this reality, this rot, this depravity would at last come to light.

The Wager continued to sail for the time being.

The greatest threat to them was no longer the sea.

As the storm continued to rage across The Wager's deck in late March, a more subtle and subtle storm that was invisible from the crow's nest and unabated by sails was tearing through the ship from within. Silently, it slithered through bone and flesh, creating memories of the living and monsters of mankind.

Walter Elliot, the ship's new surgeon, arrived from The Trial after Ettrick had been moved to the Centurion. He was lively, giving, and unusually powerful, according to John Byron, a guy who seemed to have been made to withstand the worst. With his sleeves rolled up and his mouth set, he moved with purpose and speed, devoted above all to Captain Cheap, who was now also succumbing to the illness. Elliot said, "It was a very great misfortune that our captain should be ill at such a time."

He tried everything: prayer, poultices, and tonics. The cures that were available, however, were essentially superstition masquerading as science. A man buried up to his chin in earth could be purified of all ailments, according to those who still believed in the mysterious healing power of the land itself. As tragic as it was humorous, another sailor remembered seeing "twenty men's heads stuck out of the ground." Others used Dr. Joshua Ward's notorious "pill and drop," which was promoted as a panacea. Determined not to ask his men what he would not bear, Anson took the pill himself first. Its effects were instantaneous and disastrous.

Many men who took the medication were seized "very violently, both by vomit and stool," according to Thomas's notes. After receiving a single dose, one sailor started to bleed from his nostrils and was on the verge of passing away. It would become out that Ward was a charlatan. Toxic amounts of antimony—and possibly arsenic—were included in his miracle pills. Instead of recuperating, they drained the body of its remaining vigor.

And yet the real remedy was so easy. Limes. Lemons. anything that contains vitamin C.

The invisible killer of the seas, scurvy was a monster that was brought about by a shortage of raw fruits and vegetables rather than by sabotage or storms. The body stops producing collagen, the substance that holds bones, skin, and blood vessels together, when vitamin C is deficient. Teeth fall out. Old wounds reopen. The mind breaks down.

Later, Lieutenant Saumarez admitted that he felt they had been deprived of something essential. Without certain earthly components, he wrote, "there is a je ne sais quoi in the frame of the human system that cannot be renewed, cannot be preserved... in plain English, the land is man's proper element." They had passed a lime grove back at St. Catherine. They had been close to the very salvation they required.

But it was gone now.

As if their lungs were filling with water without breath, Byron watched helplessly as the men started to gasp like drowning victims. Before they even made it to the deck, a few perished. Others collapsed after walking for a while. Many people who were transported in hammocks never reached their final destination.

According to Millechamp, "burying eight or ten men from each ship every morning was more frequent than anything else."

Eventually, 300 of her 500 men would be listed by the Centurion as "DD"—Discharged Dead. Three-quarters of her company were buried by the Gloucester. 290 people were lost in the Severn. Her team is almost half gone from the Trial. Byron saw the Wager's number drop from 250 to less than 220, and eventually below 200.

And those that were left? Stumbling, hollow-eyed, and too feeble to stand. One officer wrote, "We could barely walk along the deck." It was a chorus of spirits, not a team.

There were so many rats belowdecks that it was hard to believe they were there. They swarmed over remains left for burial, gnawed through hammocks, and scurried across food stockpiles. They ate the flesh from the deceased's cheeks. They consumed the eyeballs.

The rest of the cops, including Byron, did what they could. With icy efficiency, they entered the names of the lost into the ship's log every morning. They repeatedly penned, "Departed this life," as though words could make the truth more bearable.

Following the death of his ship's master, the Severn's captain replaced him with a young sailor called Campbell. He included the somber postscript, "I have just received notice that Mr. Campbell is this day dead," in the same letter to the Admiralty.

The midshipman Keppel, his mouth charred and toothless, became too tired to maintain track on the Centurion. "I have neglected to include the deaths of multiple men in my log," he wrote.

One entry, however, would not be overlooked.

Like a fading gravestone, it is now smudged but still readable: "Henry Cheap, AB, DD... at sea."

The young nephew of Captain Cheap. His trainee. His blood.

No storm could have gone any farther. Cheap was gutted by his loss in a manner that the illness was unable to. By his side, the youngster had been a shadow. He had now been relegated to the deep as simply another body.

Byron made an effort to honor the deceased. A funeral, a prayer, then a last dive into the ocean. However, there were too many hands and not enough. Without a ceremony or even the ringing of the bell, some were tossed overboard.

Regarding his grandfather's suffering, Lord Byron would subsequently write: "Without a grave, unknelled, uncoffined, and unknown."

The storm was still raging above them. The rats chewed below. The ship made a coffin-like creak.

And Cape Horn's rocks were in front.

They hadn't crashed yet.

They hadn't rebelled yet.

They were still awaiting trial.

However, something was already broken.

It was something no court could fix.

Something that would return to England through legends rather than ships or sails. as evidence. Actually.

And the reckoning was approaching like the waves.

After three relentless weeks of attempting to push west through the Drake Passage, the squadron was on the verge of extinction during the last days of March 1741. The water has become more ruthless and the storms more terrible. Cape Horn had evolved from a passage to be sailed to a force to be endured, a living, screaming creature that would not let them leave.

In straightforward terms, Reverend Richard Walter described it as "total destruction."

The Juan Fernández Islands, an archipelago lost in the Pacific some 350 miles off the coast of Chile, were their only hope left, located far beyond the continent's raging edge. Not a town. No harbor. Not a flag. Simply land. Beautiful, immobile, lush country. Walter stated, "The only chance we had left to avoid dying at sea was to get thither."

It meant more than just survival for young John Byron, who was half-frozen and half-starved. Legend was what it signified.

Years before, in the parlor of an English house, he had read about Juan Fernández in Woodes Rogers' Cruising Voyage Round the World, a novel that had sparked his imagination. When Rogers and his crew, ravaged by scurvy, made landing there in 1709, he spoke of a miracle encounter and discovered that the island was not, in fact, uninhabited.

Alexander Selkirk, a Scottish sailor who had been stranded for four years following a shipboard argument, lived there. Selkirk had survived on his own, with just a Bible, a knife, a gun, and a few tools. He used a nail as a needle to make a garment from skins, hunted goats, and scraped fire from sticks. He was referred to as "the absolute monarch of the island" by Rogers.

Defoe's Robinson Crusoe had immortalized Selkirk's story, which was passed down from sailor to sailor like a secret map. The island was more than just a haven to the English. It served as a tribute to their inventiveness, power, and fate.

Byron and his fellow sailors now dreamed of that long-lost island with a feverish desperation, following the storms, the famine, and the scurvy. They witnessed it while they were asleep. Its name was whispered into their hammocks. They dreamed of verdant hills, new streams, and the feel of firm ground beneath their shriveled feet. It was dubbed the "long wished-for island" by Millechamp. In his journal, Thomas likened it to Eden.

Then came an early April night.

For the first time in weeks, the winds started to lessen. The stars whispered a new route when the clouds opened just enough. Byron and the others thought they had succeeded. They discovered they were finally west of Cape Horn Island after spending over a month lost in the Horn's jaws.

The time had come.

To head north, toward the islands of salvation, was the directive.

With their sails flapping in the quiet of the moon, the ships turned together. There was happiness, tentative, fleeting, but genuine. They were moving toward freedom, toward warmth, away from the roaring south.

Then the guns arrived.

The silence was broken by two bursts from the Anna.

Something had been noticed by lookouts, something unexpected and not charted. Strange shapes appeared through the cloud in the direction they had just turned. rocks.

Not merely rocks, but towers, glittering and dark, rising from the ocean like a drowned cathedral's fingers. They stood "like two black towers of an extraordinary height," according to one captain's writing.

The crew gasped in dismay. In no way were they west of the continent.

They had been pushed back toward the landmass they thought they had fled, eastward.

They had been misled by dead reckoning. Once more.

The decks were in a panic. To swing the bows, helmsmen had to exert a lot of force. The ships managed to avoid smashing into the lee shore by turning just in time. Near enough to hear the surf roaring against them like a beast denied, the rocks went by.

However, the delusion was destroyed. The hatred of the Horn had not left them.

They have never departed from it.

They had been in the Drake Passage for over a month, and they were still caught in its whirlpool. "Our seamen, now almost all despairing of ever getting on shore, voluntarily gave themselves up to their fatal distemper," Millechamp wrote in his notebook, capturing the despondency that was consuming the crew like a layer of frost.

Worse, they started to feel jealous of the deceased.

Once supported by Robinson Crusoe's island fantasy, Byron's heart collapsed under the weight of reality. The ships made another turn, heading south into the storm's eye and away from Juan Fernández. It was a survival path rather than a strategic one.

Hope in reverse.

A descent.

They lost guys with every wave. The vision of land faded like a mirage with every wind. Some gave up completely, refusing to eat, to obey commands, even to talk. The illness worsened. The sky grew dimmer. The sea is colder.

They had ceased to be explorers. Crusoes no more. No longer British.

They were dark.

And The Wager continued to sail toward the last hush of wreckage, half dead, half crew.

_____ * * * _____

Chapter 6
ALONE

The ocean no longer behaved like water by the end of March. It no longer followed the wind or the tides, nor did it rise and recede. It launched an assault. Every gust was a statement, every swell a menace. The Horn was not done with the Wager and the rest of Anson's fleet, despite their valiant attempts to claw at the South American rim.

It was more irate now.

There was more than one storm in what John Byron would refer to as the "perfect hurricane." As though the water itself had made the decision to completely destroy the expedition, it was a series of storms, each more intense than the one before it. Screaming gales that tore at canvas and spirit were followed by walls of water, sheets of sleet, and others.

Because there weren't enough men left standing, Gunner John Bulkeley, whose sinews were formed by iron discipline, now commanded back-to-back shifts and stood watch for eight hours at a stretch. Even he, who in his journal derided the quiet Byron, now sounded like him: "We had...the largest swell I ever saw."

The entire squadron echoed the sentence. The sea was "greater than I ever saw before," according to the Severn's seasoned captain. The Pearl's George Murray agreed. Exaggeration was not a trait of these men. Language, however, had started to fail them.

Like a shattered toy, each wave threw the Wager down after swallowing her full. According to Bulkeley, the ship plunged into an abyss of darkness, with another enormous wave looming ahead, while rushing "on an avalanche of water." It was a never-ending cycle of terror—one mountain behind, another in front.

Like an ancient bone on the verge of breaking, the hull creaked. Underwater, the yards dipped. Men in the air became into insects clinging to frozen rope webs.

Then, one night at eleven, violence united the sea and the sky.

According to Schoolmaster Thomas, we were taken on the starboard bow by a furious sea. Both fore and aft, it broke in clear. With decks inundated and men tossed over her timbers like dolls, the Centurion lay flat on her side. The ship trembled, moaned, and then miraculously, gently, straightened up. She was returned by the storm.

Not everyone was as fortunate.

On The Wager, a boatswain's mate was thrown down the deck, breaking his collarbone. It broke again later. The femur of another individual was broken. A shattered neck caused the instant death of one seaman.

Not even the officers were exempt. Thomas was rendered unconscious by a wave as he attempted to adjust their position using the stars. He stated, "I came down on my head and right shoulder with such violence that I was quite stunned." For two weeks, if swinging, soaking misery could be called a rest, he lay in his hammock.

Bulkeley too came close to death. A tremendous wave took him off his feet and "carried me over the wheel" when he was at the helm. He only managed to land without breaking any bones by some miracle. One of the four valuable cargo boats, the cutter, was ripped away and flew across the deck during the same flood.

John King, the boatswain, shouted for it to be thrown overboard. But he was instructed to wait by Bulkeley, who was always the force of measured command. He warned, "Don't do anything with her." He would consult Captain Cheap.

Cheap had become more distant and authoritarian, pacing his large cabin with his silver-headed cane rapping the floor like a clock. Bulkeley, who had faith in steel and seamanship, saw Cheap as turning into a fanatic, a man who was deaf to criticism and fixated on glory. Bulkeley grumbled in his journal: the boatswain was evil, the master was a phony, the lieutenant was worthless, and Cheap was becoming more and more unstable.

Nevertheless, the captain gave the order to secure the swinging jibboom and save the cutter. Bulkeley complied, remarking with satisfaction that he had saved them both. In a ship that was quickly becoming disorganized, it was a silent display of might.

At times, the gusts were so strong that the sails had to be completely furled. The ships would then drift helplessly beneath naked poles. Anson was forced to send men into the air at one point to spin the Centurion, not to operate the rigging but to serve as sails themselves.

Spreading their arms, they used their flesh to catch the wind as their bodies froze and were whipped by the rain, their backs turned to the gale. It was successful—just long enough to move the bow. Then a topman slipped out of his hold.

He went down.

He could not be saved.

His arms slashed against the water as he rose up in the roiling sea. He swam vigorously. His jaw dropped. He disappeared once more. Then he surfaced again, behind the ship, the ocean swallowing his cries, still swimming, still striving. Reverend Walter subsequently stated, "He might continue sensible for a considerable time longer of the horror attending his irretrievable situation."

Poetry was to be inspired by that anonymous individual.

After reading the story, William Cowper wrote "The Castaway":

He washed away his floating home forever, along with his friends, hope, and all of his sorrows.

No poet shed a tear for him, but Anson's tear is wet on the page of the story that honestly describes his name, value, and age.

But the living could not be preserved by poetry.

Worms were now holding the biscuits on board The Wager together with dust. According to Thomas, they could be reduced to powder with a "little blow." The physician attempted to keep the soldiers from eating the salted beef and pork because they were so deteriorated. It was a gradual but sure poison, he worried.

There was no more fresh water. Captain Murray acknowledged on the Pearl that a mass death from thirst had only been avoided because of the scurvy deaths.

One man completely went insane. Below deck, he was shackled in irons.

Their last haven, their one barrier between the abyss and humanity, the ships themselves, were suddenly failing.

The timbers broke. The nails came loose. With each swell, the Wager moaned. They had ceased to sail. They were heading toward death, propelled by the will of an ocean that appeared determined to swallow them all, not by ambition or navigation.

They would land soon.

It wouldn't be salvation, though.

It would be disastrous.

A wreck.

Conflict between men.

And the protracted, arid court of judgment that would attempt to make sense of what could never be described in its entirety.

The sea still held them for now.

And the reckoning was rising, just like the tide.

It started with a tear rather than a yell.

The Centurion's topsail broke open like linen snagged on a nail in heaven, followed by a whispering sound that was hardly audible in the gale. Shortly after the canvas unraveled, the shrouds, the strong vertical ropes used to brace the masts, snapped like violin strings under the wind's strain.

Then the lightning struck.

According to Midshipman Keppel, it was "a quick, subtle fire" that moved over the deck before flashing like a pistol. A number of men were hurled to the boards, their limbs spotted with bluish bruises from the electric blow, their skin charred. As though about to jump into the sea, the figurehead lion, the bold crimson symbol of England's fury, started to tremble from its mount above them.

Once the squadron's jewel, the Centurion had devolved into "a crazy ship," as Reverend Walter put it.

The other ships reported their own plunge into pandemonium everywhere else.

Braces, tackles, halyards, and backstays all broke. Ladders fell apart. Hand pumps didn't work. Waves destroyed the heads, the onboard restrooms, forcing men to lean over the slippery, bucking rails or waste themselves in buckets. The stoves even failed. The captain of the Severn remarked sourly that his mending needle could not rest till his sailmaker was pronounced dead.

A few days later, Bulkeley heard the Gloucester's guns, a harbinger of impending doom. One of the main yards was split in two. Never one to put off assistance when it was required, Anson gave Captain Cheap the order to send John Cummins, The Wager's carpenter, to help. Bulkeley's best buddy, Cummins, was pulled—half-drowned—aboard the Gloucester after the gunner waited motionless at the rail and watched him ride a transport boat across vicious waves, bouncing and vanishing in the spray.

The wager was still valid.

Her lines were far from graceful, her timber was bent, and her commanders were idiots, according to Bulkeley, but she was his. He had been faithful to her for too long. She was being unmade now, though. With each swell, she let out a moan. Her hull cracked beneath the weight of years, bending like a spine. She begged to be put down because she had turned into an old beast at sea.

The mizzenmast then toppled.

There was a scream of wood, a tearing of canvas, then a thunderclap as it fell overboard, sails and all, leaving only a splintered stump in its wake. As he observed the aftermath, Thomas foresaw that a ship in this state would not be able to survive in these waters.

The Wager started to fall behind the squadron. Now she was too wounded, too slow. As the Centurion turned around, Anson used a speaking trumpet to shout across the water:

"What keeps you from setting your topsail?"

"My rigging is all gone and broke fore and aft—and my people almost all taken ill and down," Cheap's wind-torn voice replied over the waves. However, I'll set him up as soon as I can.

As soon as the weather permitted, Anson vowed to bring Cummins back. The carpenter immediately got to work jury-rigging a sail with his friends after being carried back at last. In order to give the Wager just enough impetus to continue moving, they stitched enough cloth together and tied a forty-foot boom to the mast stump.

However, it was too late. The fleet was disintegrating.

The men-of-war vanished into the mists one by one.

The first to go were the Pearl and the Severn. Bulkeley wrote in his journal, "Lost sight of the Severn and Pearl," on April 10. Some thought they had escaped to safety by turning around and heading east around Cape Horn. Thomas believed that they had done so "intentionally." Cowardice, maybe. Clarity, maybe.

Only three of the squadron's five ships were still operational.

The ships started firing signal guns every half hour and suspending lanterns from the rigging to keep what was left intact. A glimmer in the shadows. A boom under the wind. A cry for the emptiness.

Bulkeley was afraid of more than simply disease or destruction. It was a breakup.

They would lose their only chance for life, coherence, and rescue if they lost the fleet and Anson. They would be on their own in a sea that had forgotten who they were.

And the inevitable occurred on April 19.

Bulkeley saw the Centurion's last lamp that night, flickering like a dying star as he gazed over the black sea. Then it was gone.

"I never saw the Commodore again after this."

The other ships vanished into thin air as well. The wind swept their firearms away one by one. Mast silhouettes vanished into the clouds. Their sails turned to smoke.

The Wager was by himself.

No escort. No directives. No future map.

Only the quiet of the depths.

The moan of her injuries.

And the reckoning that awaited on a barren shore, where survival would require something more sinister than compliance, rather than in the next wave.

And where every decision would eventually be remembered while being sworn in and subjected to cross-examination.

------- * * * -------

Chapter 7
THE GULF OF PAIN

His Majesty's Ship The Wager's commander, David Cheap, refused to go back.

Not for the wind. Not for the wave. Not even for the deceased.

He saw his crew members deteriorate every day: scurvy-blackened skin, guys hunched over, teeth loosened in their jaws. He denied that his own physique was deteriorating as well. He said, "Rheumatism." "Asthma." He refused to give the word "scurvy" the respect it deserves. It was a failure and a stigma. And Cheap, half-deaf, emaciated, cane-tapping, and utterly driven, refused to let defeat define him.

It was more than simply devastation to the ship underneath him. She was ruined. Her hull was leaking, her sails were in ruins, and the mizzenmast was gone. The bilge smelled of death and illness. Nevertheless, The Wager, a man-of-war phantom, continued to sail.

Due to her captain's refusal to stop.

The final spark in Cheap's long-sputtering career was the rendezvous point, which was somewhere near the Chilean coast. Commodore Anson himself had given him covert orders to advance and attack the Spanish town of Valdivia, a strategic foothold on the Pacific coast. The Wager carried a large portion of the squadron's equipment. The mission could still be successful if Cheap made it to the rendezvous. It would fail if he didn't. Additionally, cheap would mean nothing.

In the logbooks, a ghost. A joke at Portsmouth's taverns.

He wouldn't permit that.

He battled the wheel, the sky, the crew, and even time itself week after week. They were now going northeast, dragging themselves along the Chilean coast, having barely rounded Cape Horn. The sea made fun of them. As though the southern ocean's gales had banded together for a final assault, storms rose once more. The supposedly tranquil Pacific turned into a seething, clawing beast.

Skeletal, worn out, and some unable to stand, Cheap's own soldiers started to grumble. As many believed the Pearl and Severn had done weeks before, some wanted to "cut and run." Cheap, however, stood firm. His face was sunken and broken by the wind. Salt and tension caused his voice to break. But he never loosened his orders. He launched them into the gusts and up the masts. He made them operate the hand pumps, repeatedly dragging saucers out of the wet hold after lowering them on chains. It wasn't labor; it was torment. Nevertheless, they complied. or acted as though they did.

Alexander Campbell, the midshipman, was his most ruthless enforcer. "I had an intense bond with the Captain," Campbell would later admit. He yelled orders and intimidated the weak. Half-delirious with exhaustion, one of the sailors swore revenge and cursed him in his face.

The bodies continued to accumulate.

"Let the fate of particular persons be what it will be," Cheap yelled into the wind. However, let our nation's honor endure forever.

Always on the lookout for natural cues, Byron saw green threads floating on the ocean below on the quarterdeck.

Seaweed.

His voice was tight with panic as he warned Bulkeley, "We can't be far off the land."

Bulkeley, who had experienced innumerable storms, didn't require explanation. In the wind, he sensed it. The salt smelled of it. They were too near. Too close.

The ship's navigator, Master Clark, maintained that they were still at least sixty leagues away. However, Clark's dead reckoning has previously proved incorrect. Charts could not quantify the cruelty of the currents.

Cummins, the carpenter, put it simply: "The ship isn't suited to enter with the land. Not when all of our men are ill.

Bulkeley approached the second-in-command, Lieutenant Baynes. "We have to go west," he said. "Go back to sea."

Baynes averted his gaze.

He murmured, "The captain won't change course," when pressed. You should talk to him.

However, the gunner had already been called in by Cheap.

Sweat, salt, and nausea filled the cabin. The ship had pitched endlessly, tossing and rearranging everything inside. The floor clattered beneath the silver-headed cane.

"What distance do you reckon yourself off the land?" Cheap said casually.

Answering calmly, Bulkeley said, "About sixty leagues, sir." Then, in a quieter voice: "But we are being pushed to the east. The ship has sunk. We have lost our mizzenmast. Our guys are down.

Cheap's expression tightened. He spoke in a bland tone.

For the first time, he disclosed the full force of Anson's directives. The Valdivia mission. The assault that still relied—unachievably—on them. They refused to stray. Not right now. Not with their proximity.

"I am obligated and resolute," Cheap declared.

That put a stop to it.

With a bow, Bulkeley walked away. He described it as "a very great misfortune" in his journal.

The cane continued to tap while the captain stood by himself, his ship creaking beneath him.

The squadron was gone behind them. The rocky coast of southern Chile lay ahead, hidden by fog and spray.

Landfall would occur.

Not salvation, though.

There was going to be a disaster.

Mutiny accompanied it.

Blood.

judgment.

And then, as the truth started to emerge from the waves, there was silence in the courtroom.

On May 13, morning arrived as a somber compromise between light and storm.

In a madman's orchestra, the Wager, beaten beyond recognition, battled its way across the raging Pacific, its masts fractured staves, its hull a wound. Young John Byron was on duty at eight in the morning when the ship moaned with a fresh break—the rigging was swinging like severed tendons as a number of pulleys on the foresails snapped.

One of the few men who still moved with any purpose, John Cummins, who was the ship's carpenter, hurried ahead to assess the damage. The thunderclouds that had covered the horizon for days began to stir just a little as he arrived at the bow. Cummins noticed something dark and crooked in that crack of gray. A form that had no place in the water or the sky.

Was it on land?

He looked more intently. It moved but remained in place. There were angular, high contours.

Lieutenant Baynes was his next target. "I think I've spotted land, sir," he said.

Baynes wiped the rain from his lashes and squinted, but he saw nothing. The vitamin shortage might have been the cause. Many people on board were half-blind by that point. It might have been smog. Baynes brushed it off. "It's impossible," he declared. He estimated that they were still 150 miles out from the coast. He didn't inform the captain.

The sky had already sealed once more, a solid mass of charcoal, when Cummins informed Byron of what he had witnessed. It was too late when Byron looked out to sea. He didn't see anything. He paused. Must he tell the captain? Baynes, however, was second in charge. And simply a midshipman, Byron. I don't belong here, he thought.

Hesitancy was chastised by the water.

With just three seamen on duty at two in the afternoon, the situation had gotten out of hand. The ship's unacknowledged spine and gunner, John Bulkeley, scaled the rigging himself to assist in lowering a yard. He scaled it—up, up, up into the rigging, where the rain ripped at his eyes and the wind slapped at his face—but the ship heaved like a beast in the middle of death.

Then he noticed it, swinging far above the deck, clinging to the yard.

Land.

Huge. Craggy. unchangeable.

It's not a mirage. Not optimism. Not a myth.

The Patagonian coastline rises from the ocean's teeth like a fortress's wall. Crippled, undersailed, and cursed, the Wager was tearing toward it.

Bulkeley clambered beneath. Rain-slick, he slid over the deck, arms braced, feet slipping, and arrived at Captain Cheap, who stood with unwavering eyes, watching the water.

Cheap made a quick move.

He yelled, "Set the foresail and sway the foreyard up."

Men who were half-crippled staggered into action. Cheap ordered a jibe, a desperate maneuver that would spin the ship and catch the wind from behind, and the helmsman, the only one fit to grip the wheel, braced against the double spokes.

The bow started arcing. Sails buckled and snapped. The ship was thrown forward too quickly and too far by the gale, which grasped the canvas like a god's hand. It headed directly toward the cliffs as it swept down the face of a massive swell.

The breeze was broken by Cheap's voice. "Keep the wheel stable!"

Against the storm, the crew yelled, strained, and pulled.

And, amazingly, the bow turned. With a whip-crack, the sails swept over. The ship finished the jibe and was now traveling south along the rocky coast.

They weren't secure.

They were confined.

The Gulf of Sorrows was this. The Penas Golfo. They had underestimated how close the shore was. Now, they were surrounded by craggy cliffs and inlets fed by glaciers. The sky was clawed at by forested hills. They were pulled inside by the currents. Winds from the west forced them to destruction.

In order to propel them farther out to sea, Cheap had the sails trimmed.

However, the final chance, the topsails, blew off the yards, shredding them like paper.

Desperation gripped the team as they froze.

So Cheap hurried onward, captain still. To lead, not to give directions. With every lunge, his silver-headed cane thudded as he sprinted toward the bow, toward the battling forecastle hands. His coat was torn by the wind. His skin ached from the saltwater. He believed that now was the time to save the ship and prove to his crew that there was still hope.

Then there was a wave.

Only one. Enough to make a step shaky.

Cheap disappeared.

A thud, a yell, a hollow sound, and then quiet.

A damaged seam in the deck had allowed him to fall through an open hatch. Straight down, six feet, hitting the bottom deck's hard oak. A crack reverberated across the hull as his body hit the wood.

The men discovered him crushed, with a pale face and an open mouth but no words.

He had broken his left shoulder. The bone went through his underarm. The flesh ripped. Slowly, blood seeped into his uniform.

He was taken to the cabin of the surgeon. He mumbled orders as he stirred, then moaned and became still.

Cheap, tenacious, enraged, and unyielding, was now broken.

Opium was administered by Dr. Walter Elliot.

And Cheap slept for the first time in weeks.

Not the command sleep. Not the grit or guilt-ridden slumber.

However, the gentle, floating drift of a man who had sacrificed all for the sea and who had been shattered like his ship in return.

The Wager slid toward ruin outside.

Her captain dreamed inside.

The rocks were also in a waiting position.

It started with a shock, so faint at first that it could have been mistaken for a wave's ghost.

John Byron was standing on deck at 4:30 a.m. on May 14, soaking through, sea-stung, and restless, when the Wager lurched violently and shudderingly. The moan, a sound of wood grinding against immobile objects, came from far below.

Midshipman Campbell, a little lad disguised as a man, spoke next to him in a voice that revealed his youth. "What was that?"

Byron sought to break through the storm's black veil by turning his face toward the wind. The bow was out of his line of sight. He briefly thought it was a wave, some terrible surge that had caught them off guard. However, no. It had not been a side force.

It had been from below.

It was a rock.

Already knowing what the sound indicated, John Cummins, a carpenter in his hut, leaped from his hammock. He hurried to check the damage after grabbing his friend James Mitchell. Mitchell vanished into the hold below, lamp swinging, as Cummins waited close to the hatch.

"No water explosion!" Mitchell yelled. "The boards are complete!"

A sigh of relief.

The sea then hit once again.

The ship struck another concealed reef as it sprang forward. A two-ton anchor burst away and blasted right through the hull, followed by a loud, tearing sound and the horrible crack of timber. Water poured in. The tide sucked the rudder away with a smooth snap.

The Wager started to list—unnaturally, heavily. Her timbers now creaked like a death sentence every time.

The sick, those who hadn't walked in weeks, rose like phantoms from below. Their eyes were wild and their skin was dark. Coughing, groaning, gripping the rails, they stumbled onto the rain-soaked deck, emerging from one deathbed to enter another.

Byron wrote later that "the Wager lay for some little time in this terrible situation, every soul on board looking upon the present minute as his last."

There was another wave.

She spun aimlessly amid snarling and howling breakers as it swept the ship. "Six feet of water!" exclaimed Mitchell, pallid and trembling, as he emerged from the hold. The ship was rapidly flooding.

A few men fell on their knees, muttering half-remembered prayers or gripping rosaries. With a bottle of vodka in hand, Lieutenant Baynes stumbled to a corner and drank without raising his eyes. Others unbound themselves. One sailor danced with his cutlass and proclaimed himself King of England. Persuaded by the sea's benevolence, another attempted to jump overboard.

Teeth chattering, John Byron gripped the rigging and watched it come to life. Beside him, a man wept for his mom.

John Jones, a weathered seaman with eyes like cannon barrels, came forward at that moment.

His voice soaring above the wind, he yelled, "My guys, let us not give up! Have you never before seen a ship surrounded by breakers? Let's make an effort to get her to finish!

He reached for a rope. "Come, help out. This is a sheet! A brace is here! We are capable of saving our lives!

It was sufficient. There was a disturbance. Bulkeley, Byron, many officers, and even some of the frantic deckhands jumped into action. They struggled to set the few remaining ragged sails, tugged at ropes, and bailed the rising water. Despite the fact that his wheel was worthless, the helmsman refused to give it up.

And the ship retaliated for a while.

She lacked a rudder. No mizzenmast. The pumps were unable to keep up. Despite this, she continued to move through the Gulf of Pain, wounded but defiant.

As though she were still alive, the men whispered her on.

Then she hit.

One last reef. The ship reared like a horse that had been stabbed.

Before they could bring the ship completely down with them, the remaining masts started to fall and were chopped off. Like a shot, the bowsprit cracked. Windows blew apart. The treenails were wooden pins that protruded like teeth from the hull. The entire building creaked and fell inward as the walls cracked and the cabins sagged.

From chamber to room, water rushed. Rats ran up in large numbers. Men in hammocks drowned where they lay, too feeble to move. They were inaccessible.

It was "a scene men do not soon forget," as Lord Byron would later write in Don Juan. that shatters their heads, necks, hearts, or hopes.

Then, amazingly, a last act of kindness.

The Wager became stuck between two enormous rocks after being flung into her grave by rage and waves.

According to John Byron's recording, "we stuck fast."

She stayed afloat. Not entirely.

She remained, half-dead but not quite gone, imprisoned like a wounded beast in a steel jaw. Overhead, the storm howled. She was still being beaten by the breakers. But she barely managed to hold.

Byron ascended to the upper deck's remnants.

The skies had cleared a bit.

And he saw it beyond the roar and the froth, past the dead and the wreckage:

An island.

obscured by fog.

Awaiting.

------- * * * -------

Part Three
Castaways

Chapter 8
WRECKAGE

The sea level was rising. As it crept slowly toward the surgeon's cabin, where Captain David Cheap lay motionless after having his arm crushed and reset only days before, it licked the corridor flooring and sounded like something living. The air was heavy with fear and salt. The scraping sound—a steady, grinding moan from below—was unmistakable, even though the captain hadn't been there when the hull struck. There was only one thing that made that sound: rock. Clear, quiet, and confident. And with it came the silent breakdown of all the goals Cheap had woven into this journey.

He was a man who had traveled across seas in pursuit of grandeur, and now it seems that the sea would reclaim everything. He hadn't mutinied, been hit by opposing cannon fire, or driven aground in combat. No, jagged, concealed stone had undone the Wager, his first command of a man-of-war. Like seawater, the irony was stinging. For this ship, Cheap had sacrificed everything. She was now dying under him.

The future, or what little might be left of it, twisted in his mind. He would be subject to a court-martial if he lived. The inquiries would be harsh. Was he careless? Willful? Had his directives been unclear, his judgment impaired? And why hadn't he been warned earlier by Lieutenant Baynes, blasted Baynes? The surgeon's silent betrayal was the most horrifying of all; the opium used to treat his fever had reduced not only his agony but also his command. Cheap would later curse, "He told me it was something to prevent fever." "To the best of my knowledge."

Then there was a knock—two midshipmen, Byron and Campbell, wet through, white as ghosts—while the wreckage of the Wager moaned and jerked against the rocks, waves breaking with the persistence of judgment itself. Like messengers from the opposite side, they stood in the doorway.

With a taut voice, Byron declared, "There is an island." Something like a musket went off. No settlement, swampy. Not a trace of life.

However, it was land. And land was salvation at the moment.

With the same measured composure he had always maintained, Cheap issued his command: "Deploy the boats." Each and every one. Help the ill. As the death rattle of the Wager thundered overhead, his face hardly moved. The cutter, the barge, the yawl, and the thirty-six-foot longboat would be the ships of salvation. If they could be rescued from the broken deck by the crew.

"Please join us, sir," Byron said.

Cheap, however, wouldn't. He served as a captain. Furthermore, a captain never leaves his ship. Not till the final man. Unless he has to drown with her. His voice was hollow with resolution as he stated simply, "Don't mind me."

A seaman with little emotion to spare, John Jones, even pleaded with him to leave. Once more, Cheap declined. "He didn't care about his own life if the lives of others were saved."

Cheap's voice had "as much coolness as ever he had done," according to Byron's later writing. However, there was also a ghostly quality to it, as though Cheap thought that sinking with the Wager may wash away the humiliation of its demise and that only death could restore his honor.

Chaos had claimed the deck above them. The ship's gunner, John Bulkeley, a man of quick thinking and gradual trust, was making a valiant effort to bring things back under control. However, no masts remained to lower the boats. Their longest lifeline, the longboat, was broken beneath the wreckage. Sailors sobbed, staggered, and cursed. A few were incapable of swimming. Not everyone would jump. Despite being lighter, the barge could be pulled. With their hands bleeding, their muscles screaming, and time slipping, Bulkeley and a few other men started pulling it across the slanting deck.

Heave! Heave! They tipped it over the gunwale and into the surf with one last pull.

Men clambered over each other to get inside. Many jumped, almost toppling it. Bulkeley saw them disappear into the fog on their way to the island, their oars tearing through the murky sea. They arrived at the beach. fell apart. lived.

Bulkeley waited for the barge to return on the Wager. It never materialized.

Once more, the sea had transformed. The wreckage of the ship was battered by rain. From the north came the wind. Death approached as the deck shook. At last, the crew lowered the cutter and yawl. First to go was the sickest. The youthful purser Thomas Harvey was able to maintain his sanity by collecting flour, a Bible, maps, a compass, and even a few culinary utensils. Their future would be these leftovers.

However, not everyone looked for help. Mitchell, Carpenter's friend, who had a murderous streak in his eyes, would not go. They transformed the deck into a tavern of the damned, along with others, such as the boatswain King, whose job it was to keep the peace. They sang through the rain, smashed kegs, and drank excessively.

They rejected fear in favor of craziness. Death grinned.

Still systematic, Bulkeley went down into the wreck to get the logbooks from the ship. These documents were essential—the Admiralty needed proof. However, they had vanished. destroyed. Not by water. by hand. Logs burned, pages torn. Sabotage. Intentional. The truth had been removed by someone, either an officer or the navigator.

This marked the start of the last chapter of the Wager, which was not just a story about a shipwreck but also about men—some brave, some low, some holding onto hope, and some drinking. There would be a reckoning for everything. A trial that would expose honor, command, and the thin line separating humiliation from survival.

And the most incriminating question of all would reverberate in the flickering candlelight of the upcoming court-martial: Who destroyed the records? Who sacrificed the truth to preserve themselves?

And did the sea, or the men who sailed her, really destroy the Wager?

Ankle-deep in the sea that had destroyed his world, John Byron slid through the debris like a shadow. Every swell made the hull moan. In order to remind himself that he had once been more than a castaway, he had come below deck in the hopes of reclaiming some of his belongings, such as clothes or letters. However, the ship was now a graveyard. Candlesticks, ripped books, half-sunk chairs, and other remnants of his past existence floated like ghosts on the rising sea. Even the corpses floated by, their eyes wide open and their mouths relaxed.

A horrible creak came from the ship's hull as he pushed more into its guts, and cold water rushed in like a judgment. When the timbers moaned, Byron realized he wouldn't be able to leave with anything. With only his wet garments on his back, he turned and clambered back onto the quarterdeck.

Even yet, he was unable to leave Captain Cheap. Fear did not pull as strongly as loyalty did. He located other cops, including Campbell, and they all waded back toward the surgeon's hut. Byron yelled as they arrived at the door.

Cheap shifted, squirming from shoulder ache. "Were the men safe?" he questioned, glancing at the soaked faces.

They were honest with him: everyone who might have been saved had been, with the exception of a few inebriated individuals who had put mayhem ahead of survival. Initially, Cheap maintained that he would remain—wait, maybe, for what was left of duty to be carried out to the very end. However, something pierced their voices and their wet, beseeching eyes. He gave a nod. He got out of bed slowly and unsteadily, holding a cane, and allowed them to support him.

Someone picked up his sea chest as they carried him across the slanted deck. It contained Admiral Anson's letter designating him as the Wager's captain. The horrible irony was that the document that had once declared his victory was now nothing more than paper floating over destruction.

Campbell would later write, "We carried him ashore and helped him into the boat."

As the survivors, 145 of more than 250, stumbled along the shore, the rain sliced at their faces. Cheap surveyed the faces, which were so emaciated and hollowed out by dread and hunger. Against the cold, this motley band of sailors and boys, carpenters and surgeons, Black seamen and white officers, who were hardly dressed, held on to each other.

Byron was only seventeen. The veteran gunner, Bulkeley, remained mute. Lieutenant Baynes stayed out of sight. The majesty of Midshipman Campbell was gone. Cozens had already started searching for a drink. Peter Plastow, the steward, John Duck, the free Black seaman, Morris, Clark and his son, the octogenarian cook, and the twelve-year-old youngster were all present. Seldom.

Other than what they could scrounge from their wet kits, there were few supplies, no fire, and no food. Yes, they had land. However, it was a false sense of security. Byron would write, "This was a great and merciful deliverance, but then we had to struggle with hunger, cold, and wetness." They had no ships, and there was no hope of rescue. There was nothing but silence on the island.

Cheap started to worry in that silence: Did they blame me?

Like an ice-soaked veil, night fell. They had no shelter on the wind-beaten beach strip. Wet and chilly, Byron and a few others dragged themselves inland in the hopes of finding refuge. Their fingers clawed at twisted vines as their feet sank into the muddy ground. Like ancient men in mourning, the trees leaned toward the ground, warped by storms.

Then a shape appeared through the trees. A dome. primitive. Ten feet or so across. An obviously man-made wigwam of sticks and brush. No indication of its builder. But there are weapons, tools, and lances inside. the existence of other people. Somewhere close by—perhaps observing.

As Byron would later write, "our uncertainty of their strength and disposition gave alarm to our imagination and kept us in continual anxiety."

But there was nothing they could do. A couple of guys slithered into the building, giving Captain Cheap room. Exposure would have undoubtedly killed him in his weaker state. "He would certainly have lost his life without such a shelter," Campbell subsequently observed.

Byron had no place there.

Outside, he lay with others in the dirt. Like decay entering wood, cold crept into his bones. Once their compass, the stars were gone. The sky was clogged with clouds. Then there was only the sound of the waves pounding on the coast incessantly. Branches swaying in the breeze. Through gritted teeth, the terrible wailing was heard.

The entire night was stormy.

Dawn did not bring any warmth. It was still raining. Byron sat up, his eyes vacant, his back hurting. He pushed himself to his feet. The castaways surrounding him followed suit. Except for three. An invalid. Two sickly men had been lying next to him. Still, motionless.

They were not awakened. Then Byron realized they were dead.

For a minute, the whole weight of the island, the wreck, the loneliness, and the death weighed down on him like a new flood as he gazed out toward the grey sea. He questioned whether they had actually avoided anything or had just moved on from one grave to another.

And a courtroom waited somewhere, in a future he could not yet envision. Men would lie, confess, accuse, or recall during a court-martial. where the truth, whatever it was, may eventually come to light once Cheap's name was compared to a letter from Anson.

But for the time being, all that existed was the island, the storm, and the steady ticking of mutiny, doubt, and starvation.

Standing close to the jagged beach, Captain David Cheap's weight was heavy on the cane he held like a staff of judgment. Thick as war smoke, the fog twisted itself along the rocky shoreline, shrouding the island and the sea in a spectral shroud. His Majesty's Ship Wager was still stuck grotesquely between black rocks, a skeletal monument to ambition undone, and Cheap could see it through this dark shroud. Every sound that emerged from the debris felt like it was accusing him.

He was aware of the impending event. Mitchell, King, and the other renegades who had refused to leave the ship were all but dead. What the storm had begun, the sea would complete. Duty, however, resurfaced in him like a lingering passion. He had to keep them from drowning. Not quite yet.

He called in a small crew and youthful Midshipman Campbell. "Send the yawl," he said. "Bring them in."

Following orders, Campbell rowed toward the direction of the Wager's shattered carcass. More chilling than any gale, though, was what he discovered on board. A floating purgatory of insanity was the deck. Like pirate lords following a mutiny, King and Mitchell had staked claims to what was left of the ship. The smell of unburied death, rum spills, and decay filled the air. "Psalms were being sung by some," Campbell recalled afterwards. Some are fighting, while others are cursing. Others were lying on the deck, intoxicated.

His boot lightly touched on a corpse. Another was lying in a pool of wine and brine, facedown. One man, leaning on the mast, had dead fingers gripping a bottle. The ship had devolved into a floating asylum where chaos, rather than authority, ruled. Campbell noticed a barrel of gunpowder—a lifeline—amid the debris. However, two sailors glared at him with twisted, hateful looks as he attempted to claim it.

"Damn ye!" they cried, hurling themselves at him while their oaths were still hot. A third then lunged with a bayonet. The blade glinted like judgment as it met the light.

Campbell didn't think twice. He turned and fled, leaving the wreck to the cursed, his party in close pursuit.

A loud explosion broke the howling wind that night as Captain Cheap lay rigid and restless in the improvised shelter, his damaged arm aching, his mind reliving every mistake and command. Like temple cannon fire, the blast sliced through the storm. Earth and limbs were thrown into the air as a red-hot cannonball whizzed over the roof of the bunker and crashed into the trees behind them.

Then there was another flash, a sharp jolt of light ripping through the darkness. The entire island throbbed like a battleground for a brief while.

Upright cheap sitting bolt. It was obvious: the renegades had fired a cannon as a warning, recognizing that the Wager would not survive another night. On board the dying ship, the men who had fought, joked, and robbed now pleaded for help.

To get them, he dispatched men. And they arrived voluntarily this time.

A peculiar and resentful procession took place as the last remaining individuals shuffled onto the shore. Silently, the castaways observed the inebriated sailors—those same men who had given up their drink order—stumbling along the beach in style. They wore the silks and lace of gentlemen over their dirty shirts and salt-stiffened pants: cravats taken from the officers' luggage, sparkling buckled shoes, powdered wigs, and embroidered waistcoats.

They appeared to be parody lords posing as nobles. Dressed as though he ruled over something more than wreckage, King, the boatswain, strode forward. Cheap's face tensed as his gaze followed every detail.

Then he moved to the front.

He moved forward, his cane hitting the sand deliberately. Even though the wind was howling all around him, it was unable to overpower what followed. Cheap screamed in rage, lifted the cane high, and slammed it on King's breast. Burly, cocky, and half inebriated, the boatswain fell under the impact.

"Rogue!" Cheap spat, his voice like a sail cracking across the air.

Nobody made a move.

The others, Mitchell and the inebriated mob, now shuddered in their stolen finery as Cheap scowled at them. A court was not required to impose a penalty on him. The court was him. The sentence was succinct: remove them. Every ruffle, every lace, every inch of dignity that was taken. Lost.

The guys were embarrassed and their finery had been thrown into the mud when Cheap was done, and they stood shivering in their sweat-stained rags. They "looked like a parcel of transported felons," Bulkeley remarked later.

Captain Cheap had made one thing abundantly evident despite his injuries, shame, and haunting:

He remained their captain.

------- * * * -------

Chapter 9
THE BEAST

Byron was going hungry. The inside of his ribs was being clawed at by invisible hands as his stomach started to eat itself. The castaways had discovered hardly nothing to eat in the days since wind and wreck had thrown them ashore. According to Byron, "the majority of us fasted for 48 hours, and some for even longer." Not a bird nested within reach, not a rodent skittered across the rocks. The island was as quiet and desolate as the afterlife. Even the sea, weird and broken by waves and fishless, had betrayed them. Byron bemoaned the fact that the sea itself was nearly as desolate as the land.

The chilly air was then broken by a shot. A seagull had been killed. It was a tiny, pathetic bird, but food. Captain Cheap, more disciplined than empathetic, gave the order to distribute it. Desperate for fire, the guys crowded, pounding wet flint against metal bits. A thin fire came to light after numerous excruciating attempts. As though searching for God, the smoke spiraled into the stormy sky.

Thomas Maclean, the ancient cook, prepared the chicken as if it were a banquet. He stirred in some of the valuable wheat they had brought from the wreck as he boiled it in a kettle that had been rescued. They shared their few wooden bowls with the thick, hot soup. Every man clutched his share as though it were sacred. Byron enjoyed every morsel.

Then the ache started.

He later penned, "Seized with the most painful sickness at our stomachs, violent retchings." The flour was spoilt. Instead of saving them, the food had poisoned them. They were weaker than they had been.

The wind howled colder and louder outside. The anguish returned along with the rains. The same island was described as "a place where the soul of man dies in him" by a British captain who passed it almost a century later. The description would have been a wonderful fit for Byron's ideas.

The men were starving, but they did not venture far. They were tethered to the coast by fear. The steep slopes, the dense marsh, the unfamiliar terrain—some of it was logical, but more than that, it was dread rooted in prejudice. Byron stated, "Our parties did not make...any great excursions because we were strongly convinced that the savages were retired but a short distance from us."

They therefore scavenged. Scraps, snails, and mussels. Now slowly disintegrating, the wreck started to expose its bowels to the waves. Even the mainmast stump washed up on shore, along with deck planks, a bell, and a chain pump. Byron searched the rubble for anything of value.

He then noticed bodies. They were returned by the sea. He described them as "horrible spectacles." bloated. Broken. A wooden cask, however, was a remarkable object amidst the chaos. He forced it open. meat with salt. He almost started crying at the fragrance.

Three days after the crash, on May 17, gunner John Bulkeley began to chew his portion of the meat. He wrote in his journal that Pentecost, the holy day when the Spirit descends like fire and "whoever calls on the name of the Lord shall be saved," is quickly approaching. But there was no fire here. Not a Spirit. Only decay, storm, and the nagging realization that there would be no deliverance.

The majority of the males were homeless. They suffered, ate, and slept outside. Bulkeley writes, "It rained so hard that it had nearly cost us our lives." "It would be impossible for us to subsist much longer," Byron said, echoing the dread. The cold persisted. Blue lips appeared. Teeth clattered. Clothes were cut like knives by the wind. Without being aware of it, a guy could freeze to death.

Bulkeley thought of something.

He carried the cutter ashore, flipped her keel-up, and supported it to create a makeshift cabin with the aid of Cummins and a few sturdy sailors. He referred to it as "to contrive something like a house." They huddled inside, thankful but shivering. He waved Byron in when he saw him aimlessly strolling along the shore. The first real flame of survival flashed inside. It was nearly painfully warm.

Byron removed his lice-infested clothing, scoured it clean, and then put it back on. Then he sat quietly with the rest. For now, they were still alive.

However, the problems did not end there. It was just getting started.

The captain's authority was already eroding, even though Cheap had regained it by flogging King and making the outlaws strip. Mitchell and his group continued to be dangerous and gloomy. Growing "murmurings and discontent" were seen by Bulkeley. The men were muttering. placing blame. We got into this because of Cheap. Cheap doesn't intend to rescue us.

And a more profound insight began to dawn: they were no longer affiliated with the Navy without the ship. Both volunteers and pressed men had stopped getting paid as soon as the wager was lost. What duty did they still have to obey when they had no ship, no pay, and no chance of getting back?

According to Bulkeley, "things started to have a new face."

The order fell apart. The hierarchy fell apart. All that was left was the query that would divide them:

Who are we if we are no longer sailors serving His Majesty?

They were now free men, Bulkeley and others argued. Not obligated to Cheap or any other officer anymore. They had been abandoned to perish while marooned and unpaid. That removed them from the chain of command, didn't it? They were now their own rulers, weren't they?

With each passing day, the shadow of mutiny loomed longer.

And the walls of a court-martial room waited someplace, but they were not yet able to see it. Some of those who did return to England would bring blades of witness, but not all would. And not just Captain Cheap would be judged when the gavel dropped.

When everything but a man's will is taken by the water, it would judge what he becomes.

Around the sputtering fires, John Bulkeley had heard the whispers, low murmurs, bitter grumbles that grew louder every night. Men whispered that they had been let down by Captain Cheap. Perhaps the Wager wouldn't have been dashed against oblivion if he had simply consulted his officers and turned around when warned. Bulkeley cautiously documented these feelings in his journal. He didn't want to look unfaithful. Carefully balancing survival and insubordination, he stated, "I have always acted in obedience to command." The fundamental reality, however, was obvious: the guys now turned to him. He had provided them with refuge. They had been fed by him. When their leader was unable to keep them warm, he did.

In his journal, he scribbled a quote from Dryden, almost in silent affirmation:

It takes more than just troops to achieve success; it need mental toughness and bravery in times of crisis.

They would require movement, food, and guidance in addition to leadership if they were to survive. Bulkeley looked at the heavens. He estimated that they were off the coast of Chilean Patagonia, roughly at 47 degrees south and 81:40 west. However, where precisely? Was the mainland a part of this damned island? It didn't seem likely. Uncertainty still plagued them. They were as hungry for information as they were for food.

At last, the weather broke. Just a little. Bulkeley organized a small group of people while brandishing his musket. Eager and restless, Byron went to another group. They had to push inland in search of food.

The terrain was harsh. Soggy and dangerous, the earth gave way under their boots. Clawing their way up forested hillsides where the trees were gnarled and dense as jail bars, they trekked through bogs and tangled grasslands. Corpses from the battlefield were strewn throughout. Roots gripped their ankles tightly. They scraped their faces and arms with thorns.

Byron pushed on, his hands raw from removing undergrowth. He was struck by the alien flora despite the pain. He noted that the iron wood, a wood with a very deep red color, and another wood with an extremely bright yellow color are the two types of wood that are primarily aromatic. However, flesh could not be replaced by beauty. The birds disappeared inland. A couple of woodcocks. A few hummingbirds. Rayaditos with thorny tails. One long-tailed meadowlark, alone. That was all.

It appeared like even the birds avoided this area.

Then there was the growl.

Temporarily alone from his group, Byron saw a bald, hideous vulture perched on a hill. He raised his musket and knelt down. He heard it at that point.

A guttural sneer, low. Then there was another sound, moist, strange, alive.

He stopped.

He subsequently remarked, "The woods were so gloomy I could see nothing." However, the roar returned, this time closer. He took off running. As he raced, branches slashed his face. They claimed to have heard it as well when he returned to the others, gasping for air and his eyes wide. Others said they saw something. A shadow. A form. A beast.

Maybe their thoughts were twisted by hunger. Or maybe there was something in those woods observing them. In any case, the men became terrified. not limited to nature. but of being the prey.

The foraging parties eventually gave up. It was an insurmountable island. dense. barbaric. Only a few woodcocks and some wild celery had escaped their grasp. Bulkeley noted gloomily, "This island produces no food." "Hardly comparable anywhere in the world, in that it provides neither fruits, grain, nor even roots for the sustenance of man," concurred Byron.

Nevertheless, they had to comprehend their confinement. A few others, including Byron, climbed the little peak that towered over their temporary camp. Steps had to be cut into the sheer hill, crawling up like ants in a desperate attempt to survive.

The final illusions were ripped away by the view when they arrived at the summit.

It was an island.

surrounded by ruthless cliffs and roaring surf on all sides. From southwest to northeast, it is almost two miles long, and from southeast to northwest, it is almost four miles wide. Byron made a lazy circle around. Nothing in all directions. No help. Not a ship. Not a trace of life. Just fog-covered hills that go on forever. Another uninhabited island to the south. The frozen Andes, spiky like a crown of doom, lie to the east. And below—like a moat around them—the waves crashed against the coast so violently that not even the most courageous would take a boat out.

This panorama of dreary breakers, according to Byron, "would deter the most courageous from making attempts in small boats."

There was no way out.

All the men brought back to camp was evidence of their desperation. Tension was building. Brooding in his sanctuary, Cheap realized that mutiny was inevitable and no longer a threat. The castaways had stepped across an imperceptible boundary, moving from command to anarchy and from sailors to survival. And a reckoning awaited somewhere over that border.

How they had survived would no longer be the question when that day arrived, whether it was in the middle of a British courtroom or in the woods.

To do so would be what they had become.

------- * * * -------

Chapter 10
OUR NEW TOWN

With a handgun in his hand, shining dully under the dim, mist-filled sky, Captain David Cheap emerged from the local shelter. He caught the castaways' attention, but not in a respectful way. Their gaze had changed, becoming more vigilant and inquisitive. It was as though a secret had been whispered between them: despite his rank and power, their captain was unable to take them out of this location. It's not cold. Not because of hunger. Not from their hope being gradually erased.

It had been less than a week since the wreck, and Cheap already felt his grip on control weakening. They couldn't all be carried by the three boats. There were few resources available to construct something seaworthy, and with winter quickly approaching, the months it would take seemed unimaginable. They were becoming weaker. Their thoughts, deteriorating. Cheap feared that their discipline would soon completely deteriorate.

Perhaps more instinctively than he admitted, he realized that something more than bravery or supplies was now necessary for their survival. It required unity. on the law. In order.

One day, science would use history to frame this battle. The Minnesota Starvation Experiment in 1945 would demonstrate that starvation could destroy humanity even among strong, moral men—volunteers, pacifists. When the subjects were denied food, they became agitated, suspicious, and aggressive. One had cannibalistic fantasies. One person made an attempt at suicide. A researcher was attempted to be killed. The final report would state, "How thin their moral and social veneers seemed to be."

The Wager's men had made the same drop, but more forcefully. They had to put up with greater chaos and less food. And there were only rocks and storms and death, no clipboard-wielding scientist waiting.

Despite his wounds and fevers, Cheap assumed control of narrative as well as men. He called the whole company together and read the Articles of War out loud while he stood in front of them like a magistrate in exile. He stated it didn't matter if it was land or sea. King's Law still applied to them. The death penalty was still applied to mutiny, desertion, and theft. They would be bound by the regulations. He would also enforce the regulations.

Food was in short supply and tempers were increasing, so Cheap decided that the wreck ought to be mined. The quarterdeck and forecastle of the Wager were just above the water, and its remains were still strewn across the reef. There were weapons, food, and tools in the submerged caverns. He refused to allow them to decay under the sea.

He selected a peculiar team to head the first expedition: the cautious, combative gunner John Bulkeley and the eager and devoted midshipman John Byron. Clever, self-assured, and becoming more and more well-liked by the crew, the latter had been a constant pain in Cheap's side. Bulkeley, however, was a survivor and a worker. And that was more important than following orders.

The captain's vigilant eye was Byron, who had put all on the line to save Cheap during the shipwreck.

As they approached the Wager's carcass, the crew set out in one of the boats, the waves pelting them. With its soul ripped out and its ribs bared, the man-of-war loomed like a battle ruin. They rushed aboard and tied up. The deck creaked under their weight, the planks giving way under their feet. Silent warnings, the sea lapped at people wedged between decks below.

Byron subsequently said, "It is impossible to adequately describe the challenges we faced during these visits to the wreck."

Barrels were discovered. Brandy. Wine. powder. They rowed ashore after heaving them back to the boat. More rum when Bulkeley forced open the captain's storage. More optimism.

More personnel were despatched by Cheap. According to Campbell, they worked on the wreck every day except in inclement weather. Their hands began to slowly dismantle the hull. They dug farther. They took out ten barrels of flour, casks of meat and pig, oats, peas, fabric, candles, shoes, socks, watches, carpenter equipment, and nails because they were wet, cold, and desperate. They were all priceless. They were all saved.

The guys adjusted when the wreck further collapsed, or "blown up," as Bulkeley put it. Blindly fishing beneath the waters with long rods equipped with hooks, they hauled up anything may sustain them.

Cheap converted a canvas into a central storeroom after they were back on land. It contained their lifeline—weapons, equipment, and rations—like a quarterdeck beneath canvas. Using a close-knit group of loyalists, including the physician Elliot, the purser Harvey, and the marine lieutenant Hamilton, he oversaw it rigorously. Every man had a weapon. Nobody went into the tent without permission. The salt air shone on guns. They searched boats. Stocks are recorded. The second-biggest sin after rebellion was theft.

Bulkeley was irritated. Cheap prevented him from continuing to salvage the wreck by moonlight. Bulkeley remarked sourly, "They would not allow the boats to go off and work by night because they were so protective of anything being embezzled." He perceived it as control rather than caution. And a missed chance.

However, Bulkeley acknowledged that things were shifting.

Strength came from the food, which was rationed with harsh economy. Byron wrote, "A slice for three men," but it was better than nothing. Cheap occasionally used wine or brandy to raise spirits. The wild celery they inadvertently ate helped to alleviate the scurvy. Mitchell and his crew were quieter but still grim. King, the once-brash boatswain, now avoided close contact.

Cheap appeared more stable. His once-hair-trigger fury has subsided. Despite his flaws and wounds, he was a commander who navigated the camp like a general in exile. He had created structure out of hopelessness and order out of destruction.

"Many would have died if it weren't for the Captain," Campbell wrote later.

Nevertheless, the harmony was fragile. Bulkeley had an advantage because of his journal writings. Cheap was always carrying his pistol. Still, the men muttered. Now, bitterness coexisted with obedience. And a question lurked, unsaid, behind every conversation:

If they could ever escape, who would they follow?

Because the castaways recognized one thing above everything else when stranded on this island between wildness and law—

This tranquility was short-lived.

For young John Byron, they had all turned into a group of Robinson Crusoes—forgotten men cast into the wilderness who survived by ingenuity rather than strength. Deprived of food and hierarchy, they now evaluated themselves on their inventiveness rather than their rank or uniform.

As with so many salvations, the finding was made by chance. Dark and slippery like drowned ribbon, a long, thin strand of seaweed clung to the rocks. It was dropped into a saucepan of water after someone scraped it free. After two hours of boiling, it became soft and palatable. It was "a good and wholesome food," according to Bulkeley. Suddenly, they were being fed by the rocks.

They started combining the seaweed with flour and cooking it in candle tallow that had melted. The outcome? The men called these oily, crispy patties "slaugh cakes." Campbell received an invitation to have sex with

Cheap himself one evening. He wrote in shock, "We had a slaugh cake of his making." "The greatest meal I've ever had on the island." By necessity, even the captain had been dragged low. Even the Captain had to make do with this dreadful stuff, Campbell observed.

The birds, the true prize, were still frustratingly out of reach. Floating and preening like ghosts of a feast denied, black-necked cormorants, white-chinned petrels, and other water birds perched near offshore. However, the boats were too valuable and too preoccupied with searching the wreck for wheat, wine, or guns to take a chance on hunting.

The men then conjured up bizarre vessels in their dreams. "Punts, cask-boats, leather-boats, and the like" were all noted by Bulkeley. A fleet of tattered ambition, sewn together with prayer and rubbish.

Richard Phipps, a thirty-year-old seaman, rose to fame. In what Byron described as "an extraordinary and original piece of embarkation," he broke open a huge barrel, tied a portion of it to logs with rough rope, and set out. He wasn't even very good at swimming. Nevertheless, he loaded a shotgun that Cheap himself had given him and paddled into the icy surf.

He would lift the gun, fire, and steady himself between waves when he saw a bird. It worked somehow. He triumphantly returned with his prize. Confident, he went further. charting. mapping. becoming a castaway of the castaways, as Byron put it.

Then one day he failed to come back.

The evening came to an end. Then another. Quiet.

Like fog, mourning settled. The sea has wiped out another name.

However, as hope started to fade on the third day, another sailor went hunting, but instead he saw something clinging to a jagged island. A man. alive.

Phipps was the one.

His improvised sailboat had been overturned by a wave. He had just gotten upon the rock by clawing. For days, he had sat there, cold, hungry, and by himself. A ghost beckoning the living. They took him home.

And he constructed once again.

He employed the Wager's oxhide, which was originally used to sieve gunpowder, this time. He made a canoe out of it by stretching it across bent poles. Reborn from debris, Phipps set sail again, this time with a craft that matched his determination.

Byron constructed his own with two friends. Crude and trembling, a flat-bottomed raft was pulled along by a lone pole. When they weren't dragging goods from the wreck or skimming across the lake looking for food—or perhaps just a sense of purpose—they used it.

Ever the meticulous learner, Byron started recording the seabirds. The broad-footed, short-winged steamer ducks snored as they preened, and he watched them. He remarked that the speed at which it went, "in a sort of half flying, half running motion," made him think of a racehorse. Even here, in the south battered by wind, life had continued to evolve.

Byron and his companions encountered an unexpected squall during one of their voyages. Their raft drifted away in the confusion, but they managed to haul it onto a rocky rock. Unable to swim, Byron could only look on in horror. One of the others, however, jumped right in. He returned with the raft. In the middle of wreckage, gallantry.

They didn't catch many birds. Their stomachs were still empty. The hard-won meals, however, were relished with a devotion that only the near-dead can understand.

Byron marveled as he gazed out across the ocean. The Royal Navy continued to patrol in stately frigates, flying their colors, and ruling like masters of empire somewhere over the horizon. And here he was, chasing ducks in a raft of junk and rope.

Never had the distance between the castaway and the crown seemed so great.

More than just a shelter, John Bulkeley was creating a whole new world. Equipped with a hammer, rope, and determination, he and the carpenter Cummins, accompanied by a group of devoted men, collected branches and reeds, arranging leaves and camlet wool on top of a ribbed frame until it resembled a long thatched lodge. Sailcloth strips were used as curtains. In a matter of days, their building—a large farmstead that dwarfed Captain Cheap's own—rose from the ground like a monument to survival, with fourteen dwellings under one roof. Bulkeley proudly surveyed it. "This is a wealthy home that, in other regions of the world, would buy a lovely estate," he wrote in his journal.

Barrels were chairs inside. Tables and planks. Bulkeley also established a sanctuary in a private area of the house, complete with a bed, a fireplace, and his treasured copy of The Christian's Pattern that he had saved from the Wager. In a place that threatened to obliterate all recollection of their former selves, he maintained a disciplined notebook, read by the flicker of flame, and prayed. He came into Master Clark's logbook one day, ripped to pieces. It supported his long-held suspicion that someone was trying to hide the reality of their failure. Bulkeley promised to document everything precisely. Under his care, history would not be lost.

The island changed. Once a jumble of tents and driftwood, it now possessed the framework of a precarious society. Byron described it as "a sort of village." Bulkeley tallied eighteen residences. There were weather-beaten shelters, thatch cottages, and lean-tos. Each group took up residence in its own area, naturally reproducing the Wager's class boundaries.

With his servant Plastow tending to him and his select few (Lieutenant Hamilton, Surgeon Elliot, and Purser Harvey) present, Cheap, ever the commander, conducted court in his own tent. Joined by Cummins and warrant officers, Bulkeley ran his lodge as a parallel captain. As though they were still on the orlop deck, Byron's rooms were packed together with the other midshipmen, Cozens, Campbell, and Isaac Morris. Together, the Marines set up tents. John Duck and John Jones were among the seafarers who established their own groups. With caution and danger, Mitchell and his group remained separate.

The encampment has vanished. Wager Island was the location.

They gave their world a name. Cheap's Bay was created on the beach. Mount Misery was now the steep hill that Byron had ascended. Mount Anson was the tall peak to the north. These titles, which were a combination of ritual and whimsy, gave the shapeless a sense of organization and temporarily restored their sense of conqueror status.

They produced life's cycles. A tent was used as a temporary medical facility. Day and night, fires burned, both to ward off the cold and to draw in a passing ship. Barrels were used to collect rainwater. Cloth scraps were sewn into garments. Just as they had done at sea, they mounted the Wager's bell and rung it when it washed up on shore to announce meals, get-togethers, and the tenuous strands of society.

Stories were spoken in the evenings. With tears in his eyes, John Jones recalled how he had pleaded to save the Wager before she hit rock, not thinking any of them would survive. The few books that were saved were read by others. In order to immerse himself in a past that still held out the possibility of greatness and return, Byron borrowed Cheap's worn copy of Sir John Narborough's Expedition to Patagonia.

However, the calm was only an illusion.

There were no more shellfish. Less and less gave the wreck. And hunger came back with a vengeance, consuming both the spirit and the gut. Journal entries turned into depressing chants: scavenging all day to get food... nocturnal wandering task... I didn't taste any bread. Weary... the cries of hunger...

Byron saw the distinction between a castaway among men and a castaway alone. He observed, "Ill humor and discontent were now breaking out apace." A guy wrestled with nature alone. He grappled with desperation—and other men—in a crowd.

With tangled beards and hollowed eyes, Mitchell's group prowled around frightening anyone who resisted and demanding alcohol. More often than not, even Byron's companion Cozens was inebriated from stealing wine. The village was getting tense.

Then the heist occurred.

The store tent next to Cheap's shelter was broken into, and flour—valuable, irreplaceable flour—was taken. Bulkeley wrote, "The store tent was broken open and robbed of a great deal." It was described as "a most heinous crime" by Byron. There was no hunger here. It was sabotage.

The violence intensified.

Mitchell rowed to the wreck one day with another sailor to scrounge. Later, Byron and a group followed in the hopes of joining. However, they discovered Mitchell by himself on the partially flooded deck, while the other man was dead. His body was motionless. He had a blank expression. Marks walked around his neck.

Nobody witnessed it. Nobody was able to demonstrate it.

Byron, however, thought so.

He suspected that Mitchell had killed the man in order to get the spoils. What was one more life worth in a country where every nail, piece of flesh, and drop of brandy could make the difference between life and death?

It was now a village on Wager Island.

However, it was a hungry and ghostly village. Of loaded firearms and muttered charges. A place where everything was in disarray, and the disarray grew longer every day.

And somewhere between the daily meals and the scriptures in Bulkeley's journal, a subdued plan started to take shape:

He would go.

He would construct a ship.

He would get away.

The world would eventually find out what had transpired on Wager Island when the trial had place and the Admiralty reviewed the documents and the evidence.

Or what one man said had taken place.

------- * * * -------

Chapter 11
NOMADS OF THE SEA

At first, there was only a smattering of white floating from the gray as the snow fell gently. The flakes then started to whirl like ash as the wind increased, adhering to limbs and piling up on Mount Misery as they flew across the shoreline like a wave of erasing. Under the apathy of nature, the planet was being wiped clean. In his notebook, John Bulkeley wrote, "We find it extremely cold, and it freezes very hard."

Winter was upon us.

However, the survivors weren't particularly uneasy about the snow.

Days before, as Bulkeley, Byron, and Campbell were sifting through the wreckage of the Wager in the hazy dawn light, three canoes had risen out of the haze—long and lean, gliding low through the water with an almost ethereal elegance. They froze, the castaways.

These were not the rudimentary rafts they had repaired using canvas and barrels. Crafted from sinew and bark, bent at the prow and stern, and fueled by fire, these were ships of heritage and design.

Flames danced steadily in clay hearths within each canoe. Men without shirts paddled with unhurried confidence, exposed to the waist under the chilly rain. Seal oil gleamed on their skin. Cloaks made of animal hide and braided feathers hung over their shoulders. Salt and storm had slicked their long black hair. They had lances, harpoons, and slings with them. Many dogs sat on guard between their legs, patrolling the beach like soldiers.

Chilled to the bone in his own coat, Byron gazed in wonder at their fortitude. He wrote that their attire consisted solely of a small piece of animal hide around their waists.

The strangers returned the stare.

Their eyes were full of curiosity, caution, and maybe something older, but no recognition. They had never seen such individuals before, as Byron pointed out, "and it was evident from their great surprise and every part of their behavior."

These were the sea nomads known as the Kawésqar, or "people who wear skins," who had spent hundreds of years in Tierra del Fuego and Patagonia. They weren't discarded. They were at home.

The Kawésqar saw abundance where the English saw devastation. They knew where to collect mussels, where seals mated, and where whales would beach themselves because they read the coastline like a novel. The canoes were frequently steered by women rather than males. They lived in motion rather in fortifications, hunted with bows strung from sinew, and fished with lines of seal tendon. Their home, their haven, and their hearth was the canoe.

They used fire and bone to make their implements. Harpoon points were made from whale ribs. The jaws of dolphins become combs. Bark was a bowl, a torch, and a container. Water was carried by seal bladders. Limpets were used as bait. They blinded the cliff-dwelling birds with fire at night so they could club and cook.

They didn't dress in heavy clothing. Rather, they applied blubber to their skin, maintained fires in all types of weather, and transmitted survival skills in the same manner as others did prayer.

NASA would research their methods even decades later in the hopes of learning how to survive in a colder environment.

Bulkeley, Campbell, and Byron beckoned the canoes ashore with their hats. Theoretically, the King of England had sent a telegram to Anson's voyage, promising to "rescue" any native peoples they came across from ignorance and teach them how to be "happy people." Now, however, it was obvious who needed to be rescued as Byron and his frostbitten friends stood waving fabric, wet to the skin and hungry almost to blindness.

The Kawésqar paused for a moment.

They had undoubtedly heard tales of Europeans, even if they had never seen them before. Of Magellan, who used trinkets to entice two adolescent giants onto his ship before slapping them in shackles. Of conquistadors who carried iron in their hands and disease in their breath. The deceased were renamed and referred to as salvation by white men.

Nevertheless, the Englishmen gestured for peace. A bolt of cloth that had been recovered from the wreck was offered by Byron. The rain sliced between them like a veil as the paddlers drew closer, hounds snarling low. Byron found their silence startling. He wrote, "They didn't say a word in any language we had ever heard."

The Kawésqar eased their canoes ashore after accepting the gifts.

Silent and cautious, they dragged the long boats out of the waves and stepped onto Wager Island. They were escorted by Byron and Campbell into the odd little village, which was made up of a collection of half-canvas, half-driftwood shelters that were all in desperate need. The Kawésqar surveyed the area, taking in the smoke, the bells, the rags, and the people who had rebuilt this place from rubble. They were then presented to Captain Cheap, who strangely now lived in a home similar to theirs.

There was no imperial greeting. No dominion declaration. It was only a meeting, one group attempting to survive, the other just getting by.

Nobody knew how the encounter would turn out. But in that freezing instant, beneath snow-choked skies and next to flames fueled by prayer and bird feathers, the distinction between savage and civilized became hazy.

A village had been constructed by the castaways. A globe had been mapped by the Kawésqar.

Men in warm rooms and powdered wigs would soon try to ascertain which survivors had maintained discipline, which had broken it, and what, if anything, had really set them apart from the "savages" in a court far from this forgotten shore.

When the Kawésqar returned, Captain David Cheap was taller than he had been for weeks. He was half-starved and frostbitten, but he greeted the strangers with a ceremonial formality. He was aware that these individuals might be the key to both survival and deliverance. They were aware of safe waters, secluded coves, edible resources, and the best places to avoid Spanish outposts. Their boats were seaworthy and elegant, gliding across the water like shadows. Most importantly, they had food.

The finest luxury the wreck could provide was a scarlet soldier's coat and a sailor's hat, which Cheap gave to each of the Kawésqar men. Despite the courteous reception of the presents, the clothes were not worn for very long. English cloth was of little use to the Kawésqar, who were dressed traditionally and painted in red mud. But they were mesmerized by the mirror—the mirror. One man turned around behind the glass to see the stranger staring back at him as he inspected his reflection. "The novelty had an odd effect on them," Byron wrote. For his part, Cheap remained calm and courteous. Campbell observed that the Kawésqar themselves were "extremely courteous in their behavior," and that "he treated them with great civility."

The Kawésqar then disappeared once more, disappearing as abruptly as they had appeared, gliding back over the gray lake as the blue smoke from their canoe fires faded behind them like the final vestige of hope.

They came back two days later.

They brought gifts of their own this time, including three sheep, which were not usually eaten by the Kawésqar. Both Bulkeley and Byron came to the conclusion that they had to have exchanged them for them with another indigenous group that was in communication with the Spanish up north. But it was amazing how quickly they had done it across such dangerous ground. They also brought the greatest mussels either Englishman had ever tasted, which were the size of a man's palm.

It had an electrifying effect on the castaways. Food. Actual food. "Many educated Christians found these individuals to be a good example," Campbell said.

More Kawésqar then came back. Children, women, and men. There were over fifty of them. Attracted by something older and more communal, in addition to curiosity. For them, a wrecked ship was a source of material, stories, and change, much like a beached whale. And they started building in that spirit.

In a couple of hours, Byron gazed in amazement as the homes he had called at began to take shape. tall branches anchored to the earth. The tops were removed with teeth, twisted inward, and tied with supple-jack. Over the frame are layers of bark and bux. low entryway protected with fern curtains. Once more, ferns were used as bedding. A hearth sits in the middle.

It worked well. Classy. and silent.

The Kawésqar did not recoil when one of the Englishmen was killed. They assembled in deference. sat quietly next to the body. Covered it carefully. The Kawésqar stood motionless and in awe as the English whispered their prayers. Bulkeley noted, "They were very observant and attentive." Two civilizations briefly knelt next to the same mystery.

However, the Kawésqar continued to give.

Harvested from the frigid depths, they reappeared with baskets of sea urchins after vanishing into the surf. With a basket between her teeth, one woman went into the water, had "an amazing time," and came up with a bounty, according to Byron. The yolks were a revelation—sweet, rich, and sustaining—orange and soft within their spiky shells.

The English were amazed at the methods they used to catch fish. using dogs to herd them. forcing them into nets. Bulkeley wrote, "Very surprising and unknown anywhere else."

There was no hint of dread on their faces.

But maybe they ought to have.

The castaways had started to deteriorate once more. The carpenter's buddy Mitchell and his group went back to their old ways of stealing alcohol, concealing weapons, and disobeying rules. They started to infringe on the Kawésqar's goodwill by drinking, partying, and, worst of all, chasing their women, disobeying Cheap's orders.

Byron looked on uneasily. He claimed that it "gave the Indians such offense" when they attempted to woo the Indian ladies. It was easy to see the Kawésqar observing the English with increasing skepticism. They were neither hunters nor fishers. To keep warm, they had to undress. They were fighting among themselves. They appeared to be constantly in danger of disintegrating.

Then the idea spread that Mitchell and his men intended to escape the island by stealing the Kawésqar's canoes.

Cheap took swift action. Byron and others were sent to stand guard. The Kawésqar, however, had had enough. When they had the sea, they didn't need soldiers to guard their boats.

Cheap woke up one morning to quiet.

The fires were chilly. The shelters are no longer there. They had even taken the bark.

Only recollection remained when the Kawésqar disappeared, vanishing in the night.

Byron said, "They had taken everything they had brought with them and stripped the bark from their dwellings." The gift that was presented to the castaways had not been honored. "They would have been very helpful to us if we could have entertained them as we should have," he thought.

However, the moment was over.

With their fire, their wisdom, and their peaceful dignity, the sea nomads had returned to their world, leaving behind a camp that was once more divided, once more hungry, and once more on the verge of anarchy.

And they wouldn't come back this time.

------- * * * -------

Chapter *12*
THE LORD OF MOUNT MISERY

The dog was half-starved and quivering in the chilly woods close to the camp when Byron accidentally discovered it. The Kawésqar must have owned it, but they must have forgotten or abandoned it in their hurry as they went in silence. It didn't flee when it spotted him. Step by step, it accompanied him back through the snow before curling up against him in the dark and sharing its warmth with him like a secret.

It was always by his side after that.

Byron stated, "This creature became so devoted to me that he would allow no one to approach... without biting them." It was the one creature he could fully trust on the island. The dog was his companion, his protector, and the one thing holding him to kindness amid the crumbling world of Wager Island.

But this was no place for tenderness.

The Kawésqar had vanished. Food was disappearing. Captain Cheap started reducing the already limited rations after being forced to make an impossible decision. Giving less was tantamount to inviting insurrection; giving equally was tantamount to inviting famine. The latter was his choice. For three men a day, flour reduced to one pound. Less than a few days later.

Desperate, Bulkeley led a group to the lagoon where the Kawésqar used to perform miracles. The water, however, was now empty. He wrote, "Shellfish are very scarce." "It's really difficult for us to live now." Then the weather completely changed against them. Their faces were battered by sleet. The rain turned to ice. Bulkeley observed that "a man will pause whether he shall go out in quest of food, or remain in his tent and starve."

Byron heard the growl one day while he was sitting in his shelter with the dog snuggled up at his feet.

In the entryway stood a bunch of seamen. They had wild eyes. They had flat voices.

He was informed that they required the dog.

For what, he inquired?

To eat, they instructed him.

He begged. He pleaded. He could have pleaded with the waters.

The dog was pulled away. It twisted and yelled but was unable to escape.

How it was slain was not described by Byron. Not fired. Perhaps stabbed. strangled, perhaps. He could tell anything from the silence that followed.

He later observed the men roasting the meat over a fire from a distance. As they chewed in wild desperation, shadows flickered on their faces and their eyes gleamed in the smoke.

Finally, he came over. took a portion. consumed the paws. consumed the skin.

He admitted that "our men were driven to their wits' end by the pressing calls of hunger."

Lord Byron would capture the occasion in rhyme centuries later, immortalizing his grandfather's suffering:

Thus, despite Juan's cries, his spaniel was killed and divided for today's consumption.

Soon after, the outpost's structure fell apart.

Nine resentful and armed men, including Mitchell, separated from the group. They moved kilometers away to set up their own base and became the seceders. Cheap's rule was no longer accepted by them. They pilfered food. stolen firearms. There were even rumors that they might raid the main camp if they become that desperate.

Then, while foraging on Mount Misery, a seaman disappeared.

He was discovered by a search party, his body crammed into the undergrowth and stabbed multiple times. robbed. mutated. For the crows.

Byron had no doubt that Mitchell had murdered him.

At least two murders were committed. Perhaps more.

Wager Island had always been a place to bury the dead. It was a source of human pride. Byron was afraid they would be haunted by the ghosts of the dead. This time, however, the search team left the body in its current state. The words were not spoken. Nobody was able to look each other in the eyes.

The outpost was falling apart. There were warring tribes now, not just groups.

The boatswain Sneering at Cheap's power, John King spearheaded open opposition against him. He referred to him as conceited, unyielding, a shipless captain, and an idiot who was still holding onto a seaweed crown. In accord, the men muttered. Why ought Cheap to be in charge? Here, who had given him dominion? On this rock, there was no Admiralty. No flag, only ruin.

Even Cheap's former comrade, Marine Captain Robert Pemberton, split from his troops. Pemberton asserted independent authority because they were Army and now on land. He constructed a wooden throne in his tent and sat like a general with men armed around him. A frayed flag fluttered boldly above his shelter.

Campbell wrote, "A state of anarchy is descending upon us." "It is completely unclear what the potential consequences could be."

Byron retreated to the outside of the hamlet because he was tired of the fighting. He wrote, "I built a little hut just big enough for myself, and I didn't like any of their parties."

Once more, alone.

The old ranks were no longer relevant. Everything had been flattened by the Wager's catastrophe. Death, hunger, and winter didn't care about medals. Nevertheless, one guy prospered in this democracy of sorrow.

Bulkeley, John.

He kept up his refuge like a stronghold. cleared the surrounding vegetation. gathered wood. hoarded tools and clothing. He discovered that everything was traded, bartered, and leveraged. Bulkelcy had created a currency out of garbage, but money was worthless. He kept foraging. He kept ammunition and firearms in secrecy.

He cautiously went outside each morning while holding his Bible: The Christian's Pattern. The Devil, he thought, never slept. He couldn't either.

A growing number of men approached him.

Bulkclcy and Cummins were secretly removed by Pemberton, who was once perched high on his fictitious throne. "Lieutenant Baynes is nothing," he muttered. And inexpensive? "In the same illumination."

The marine's loyalty had changed.

The focus had shifted to Bulkeley, the gunner, the outsider, the sea lawyer.

He was going to be something else soon.

The escape architect.

From within, Captain David Cheap was being eaten.

It was stealing, not hunger, though that stalked every waking moment. Their last source of income, food, was disappearing into thin air. The shop tent was being broken into by a number of people who were stealing meat, flour, and morsels. They gnawed away at the group's collective hope like rats under the canvas. Bulkeley referred to them as "vile practitioners." The castaways used a harsher term: traitors.

Every disappearance bred mistrust like mold. Men started glancing at one another with muted anger. Messmates became distrustful. Once maintained by necessity and discipline, loyalty started to wane. And a captain who was unable to maintain discipline was the only thing worse than a tyrant for sailors.

Cheap was that man, according to many now.

It was suggested by others that the food be transferred to Bulkeley's shelter. He didn't request it. Even his quiet, though, was a message. He had a roof. He was equipped with tools. He had supporters. He continued to believe.

Cheap retaliated.

He established a new rule that all marines and officers would alternately watch over the shop tent. Nobody is exempt. Not even Bulkeley, who was made to stand night watch by himself in the icy darkness—a stark reminder that he was still beneath everyone, regardless of how popular he was. Bulkeley said that there were strict directives to maintain "a watchful eye."

Even Byron had to take his turn in the dark hours after a long day of scrounging the ground for sustenance. He was still afraid of the monster, a big, silent beast that was supposed to haunt the island. When he opened his eyes, a large, clawed object was staring at him, and one seaman vowed that he had woken up to its breath on his face.

Byron's blood froze when he heard a moving within the tent one night. With his heart pounding and his weapon ready, he slithered forward. Pulling back the flap, he saw a man instead of a beast. His own. A fellow sailor. caught in the act.

After tying the robber's hands to a post, Byron called for the captain.

Punishment came quickly after.

The individual was imprisoned. Thomas Harvey, the armed purser, soon saw another figure scuttling through the bushes next to the shop. Rowland Crusset was one of the marines. He had a hunk of steak beneath his coat, enough flour for 90 men, and more concealed in the brush when he was searched. Thomas Smith, another marine who was on duty at the time, was taken into custody as his accomplice.

The camp burst into flames. Cheap referred to the theft as "starvation-by-deception." "They ought to die," he declared. Nobody disputed him. "This was… the sentiment of every person present," Bulkeley wrote.

Cheap, however, complied with the Articles of War. A trial would take place. The customs of empire would be performed even here, stranded outside of maps and compassion.

They gathered a makeshift court-martial. Rag-clad officers stood in judgment. Witnesses vowed to tell the truth. The defendant acknowledged that they had acted in order to eat and stay alive.

They were convicted.

They were spared death because the statute stated that the offense "did not touch life." Six hundred lashes, two hundred a day for three days, was the cruel punishment. Any more would simply kill a man.

It started with hail.

After being stripped down to the waist and shackled to a tree, Crusset was led forward. First came the ice. Next, leather. One sailor later commented, "The back looks unnatural after two dozen. resembles almost blackened grilled beef.

The man with the whip wore himself out. He was replaced by another. The screams were terrible. Crusset fell when the last stroke landed.

Day two then arrived.

And the third day.

After it was finished, they were banished—rowed to a desolate island and abandoned to the weather and snails. A haunting sentence.

However, the thefts continued.

Four more flour bags vanished. Four brandy bottles. The marines' tents were ripped apart by an enraged mob. They charged nine. Five of them joined the seceders in their flight. The remaining four were banished and whipped.

Then it occurred once again.

A man who stole was flogged. He was to be taken to the islet by Byron. He wrote, "We... patched him up a bit of a hut." They started a fire. I left him alone. Byron came back a few days later. The man was rigid. Lost. Ash and wind were all that remained.

The violence had ceased to astound. It beat. It expanded.

Cheap thought he had put things back in order. He wrote, "I tried to instill in them a sense of responsibility and reason." But Wager Island had long since been abandoned by reason. Hunger, resentment, and the recollection of rules that once made sense aboard floating ships under meaningful skies were all that remained.

This island, this prison of cold and treachery, had turned into a place where stealing was the only way to survive and the law meant suffering. when all hungry bellies questioned leadership and allegiance was penalized.

Thus, the true power changed behind the trials and slaps.

Bulkeley came out of his shelter every morning. The men approached him. They observed him. They muttered. And he would soon provide a means of escape, not justice or atonement.

And the upcoming court-martial would teach the world how many facts may be hidden in the snow.

------- * * * -------

Chapter 13
EXTREMITIES

The wind had just changed and torn back the veil of mist when Captain David Cheap saw the faint white trail close to his home. He initially believed it to be dust or snow, but he knelt, touched the faint line with his finger, and then brought it to his nose.

Powder.

Like a candle waiting for fire, it made a silent arc over the ground toward his shelter. With a cane trembling in his fist, he slowly rose up. Had it just happened to spill? Or had it been set on fire by someone?

Byron had heard rumors that Mitchell and his group of separatists had returned to camp while it was still dark. Rumor has it that their plan was nothing less than assassination. Byron claimed that "one who had some bowels and remorse of conscience left in him" had a hard time dissuading them. However, regret might disappear like smoke. Cheap was left to ponder whether there would be no such savior the next time.

The captain was unsure of whom to believe.

The truth was decaying more quickly than the shops. Feed by fear and honed by hunger, rumors merged with reality. Cheap was suspected of betraying not only the rabble but also the individuals he had previously trusted. According to Cheap, Captain Robert Pemberton, the marines' commander, had "lost all sense of honor." Every breeze caused Lieutenant Baynes to bend. King, the boatswain, was expelled from his own cottage for causing too many fights.

There was John Bulkeley after that.

As a man of "the people," the gunner always spoke gently. However, he welcomed defectors, hosted meetings in his spacious shelter, and provided warmth, food, and advice. No, he hadn't deposed Cheap. He just pretended that he already owned the island.

Amid the clamor of wind, hail, and surf, Cheap paced around the camp during the storm. He recalled the day Anson had appointed him captain. His victory had been that. His honor. His opportunity to steer—not merely a vessel, but a legacy.

He was now imprisoned in a ghostly and rebellious village.

He would later admit that he was plagued by "the repeated troubles and vexations" that seemed to hit him like surf against a rock, causing him to become obsessed and sleep deprived. The captain was "jealous to the last degree" of his power, "daily declining, and ready to be trampled upon," according to Byron, who was watching him with increasing uneasiness.

Everything culminated on June 7.

Cheap gave Midshipman Henry Cozens a straightforward directive: roll a pail of peas along the beach and into the store tent. Unsteady from drinking, Cozens objected. He murmured, "The cask is too heavy," and started to go.

Cheap accused him of being intoxicated and yelled after him.

"With what should I get drunk, unless it be with water?" Cozens retorted.

It was disrespectful. blatant, open defiance.

Cheap screamed. "You scumbag! Roll up the cask and get extra hands.

Cozens feigned a call for assistance. Nobody responded.

Across him, Cheap's cane cracked. Cheap then gave the order to have Cozens restrained in a tent while being watched. Bulkeley noted, "The Captain confined Mr. Henry Cozens, a midshipman, on this day." "Drunkenness was the fault that was alleged against him."

The punishment, however, did not end there.

Cheap paid the prisoner a visit that night. Cozens blew up. The camp was ripped apart by his curses. He referred to Cheap as a despot. A shame. Even worse than Shelvocke, the infamous pirate.

He spat, "Shelvocke was a rogue, but not a fool." And you are both, by God.

Trembling with anger, Cheap lifted his cane. If the sentinel hadn't intervened to stop him, he might have immediately beaten Cozens to death. "Don't hit any of your prisoners," the man added.

In a rare moment of self-control, Cheap gave in and let Cozens go.

The midshipman, however, was given additional alcohol by others. Once more intoxicated, he quickly got into a battle with Cheap's best ally, the purser, Thomas Harvey. Byron, who had always been fond of Cozens, now felt that those who wanted to push Cheap over the edge were using him as a weapon.

Then the shot was fired.

That day, it was pouring rain. Mount Misery slithered with water. Cozens waited for their rations. He heard a whisper: Cheap was going to cut his wine.

He shouted and lunged at the store tent, furious. Harvey pulled out his flintlock handgun, still resentful of their previous meeting.

Cozens continued to arrive.

Harvey leveled the barrel and cocked the hammer. "You canine!" he yelled. "Mutineer!"

As the weapon fired, another man smacked it upward. The attempt was unsuccessful.

Cheap, his pistol already pulled, dashed out of his hut.

"Where is that bad guy?"

In the crowd, he spotted Cozens. walked directly in his direction. As Cheap put the pistol against Cozens's cheek, the rain trickled down the barrel.

Then, silently, he squeezed the trigger.

------- * * * -------

Chapter 14
AFFECTIONS OF THE PEOPLE

Like a thunderclap, the sound ripped through the early mist. John Byron ran out of his dilapidated hut, his feet digging into the soggy ground. Henry Cozens was sprawled on the muddy ground in front of him, his face twisted, blood streaming from his cheek, and he was not moving. "His blood was weltering," Byron would write afterwards. Standing close by, with a pistol still smoking in his shaking palm, was Captain David Cheap. Cozens had been hit in the face by the bullet. Cheap had sought to stifle disobedience. He had cold-bloodedly shot a man, his own cop.

A few members of the stranded crew recoiled in shock at the captain's insanity as well as the violence. Since the HMS Wager had sunk, they had watched Cheap fall apart, famished and soiled. However, this? There was more to this.

Byron knelt next to his companion in spite of the stress. He took Cozens's hand as the rain trickled down his back. The child, who was hardly older, opened his mouth to speak, but all that came out was blood. With a glimmer of insight in his eyes, he glanced at Byron and gave his hand a light squeeze. Then nothing. The sound of the rain hissing and the frightened muttering of men who had long since forgotten the world of rank and regulations.

Quickly, word got out that Cozens had been shot by the captain without cause. Cozens had displayed disdain, but he had been unarmed, according to Bulkeley, the ship's gunner and unofficial head of the burgeoning resistance. No danger had existed. Tyranny was the result of Cheap's paranoia.

The guys gathered under the dripping trees as Cozens's lifeless body was brought to the temporary sick tent. Cheap, exhausted and enraged, called them to a meeting. His final supporters, Lieutenant Hamilton and the surgeon Elliot, were standing next to him. Cheap faced the mumbling line of seamen, still holding his weapon.

His voice was scratchy but forceful as he declared, "I am still your commander." "All men should go to their tents."

There was a gasping pause since a rejection may have led to insurrection. However, the men complied, their eyes downcast and their fists clenched. Resentment hung heavy in the air, "smothered for the present," according to Byron's later writing. What little order left among the wrecked had been perilously close to being destroyed by the gunfire that hit Cozens.

A silent battle for Cozens's life broke out within the sick tent. The young surgeon's companion, Robert, examined the wound. After entering Cozens's left cheek, the bullet burst through his upper jaw and lodged beneath his right eye. No wound of escape. No anesthesia. Only faith, clamps, and knives.

Robert got ready to operate the following morning. However, the chief surgeon, Elliot, did not show up. Rumors circulated through the camp in whispers. Some claimed that Captain Cheap had prohibited Elliot from assisting Cozens, while others claimed it was an old hatred. According to Midshipman Campbell, no such directive had been issued. On the island, however, reality had turned into a flimsy flame.

Bulkeley subsequently stated, "This was viewed as an act of inhumanity and greatly contributed to his [Cheap's] loss of the people's affections."

Robert braved the procedure alone. The equipment was dirty and primitive. The process was excruciating. Cozens, however, amazingly made it through it. The majority of the bullet was removed. He was far from saved, though. His face was broken, and he had lost a lot of blood. Like a vulture, infection hung in the air.

He pleaded to be placed with pals at Bulkeley's hut. Cheap, however, declined.

Cheap declared, "I will take him as a prisoner to the Commodore and hang him if he survives."

Robert conducted a second operation on June 17 to remove the remaining bullet fragment and jawbone splinters. Robert was then summoned by Cozens to deliver a package to Bulkeley. Inside: the pieces of his skull that were taken out. A lead and flesh message. The gory tokens, which were proof of command gone insane, were retained by Bulkeley.

Cozens passed away on June 24, a week later. "Fourteen days after languishing," Bulkeley noted in his logbook. They had no words to describe what they had seen, only the quiet of men who had been betrayed as well as survived.

His remains was taken to another unmarked grave in a muddy field. No ritual, no belongings, and no money to send to a family on the other side of the globe. Only hands, mud, and sorrow. "We buried him as honorably as possible given the circumstances, time, and location."

The vultures circled, but Cozens eluded them. Not quite yet.

They had spent 41 days stranded.

And a reckoning had started somewhere in the shadows of that bleak land.

------- * * * -------

Chapter 15
THE ARK

When the first glimmer of redemption illuminated the stranded's eyes, Cozens's corpse had only begun to chill in the ground. In the midst of the mud, starvation, and muttered rebellion, a new obsession developed: escape, not retaliation, not survival on its own. It came from Cummins, a carpenter whose rough hands and fevered intellect provided a strategy that no captain's order or sermon could.

Beneath the ruins and salt, deep beneath the Wager's wreck, was a longboat, cracked and half-rotted but still intact enough to inspire the impossible. It might become their ark if they could raise it, rebuild it, and make it into something more. Of desperation, not of covenant. of liberty.

Meanwhile, Captain Cheap had disappeared into his own type of debris. He was cooped up inside his hut, brooding alone while battling the ghost of Cozens. Would the Admiralty have deemed his behavior just—or branded him a murderer—had they witnessed the blood on the sand? The men had stopped trusting him. To make matters worse, Bulkeley observed that he had lost "any composure of mind."

But Cheap roused when the carpenter's plot came to light. Then, with an almost manic zeal, he plunged himself into the project. It was the only way out of exile and, possibly, the only way to forgiveness. Finding the boat, which was caught in the Wager's wreckage, was the first challenge. Boring a hole in the sunken ship's very side was the only way to release it. The group persevered through the dangerous and grueling work because they were hungry and hopeful. Like the whale's bones, they hauled the broken ship ashore.

It was not seaworthy at all. It appeared more like a ghost than a lifeboat—waterlogged, splintered, and too small to accommodate even one-third of the castaways. Cummins, however, saw not only what it was but also what it had the potential to become.

He determined that the thirty-six-foot hull needed to be extended by a minimum of twelve feet. To weather the open sea, a second mast would be needed. The majority of the wood needed to be replaced because it was worthless. The tools were simple: an adze, a saw, and a hammer. Limited supplies. The biggest shortfall, however, was time.

And hands.

Both Mitchell and Oram, Cummins's carpenter's pals, had joined the separatists. Mitchell was insane. Oram, though? He could still be reclaimed. In order to get him, Cheap devised a secret plan and sent a small crew across the cliffs and thickets of the island. Always strategic and cautious, Bulkeley was selected to spearhead the assault. He would write, "I had to act very secretly in this affair."

They waited for Oram to separate from the others when they arrived at the seceders' camp. They then offered to return to the fold, assist in building the ark, and be pardoned while hiding behind low trees and loaded muskets. Oram paused, possibly weighing hanging death against hunger death. However, hope is difficult to eradicate, much like rot. He consented to return.

The beach was buzzing with activity by the middle of July, three weeks after Cozens's passing and two months after the catastrophe. Nothing felt more essential to moving our delivery forward from this barren location, according to Byron. The groan of lumber beneath the saw was the sound of Hope's rhythmic discovery.

Under Cummins' supervision, the boat was cut in half and placed on wooden blocks for each half. Then came the miracle: reassembling the fragments into something bigger, bolder, and reborn rather than just as they were. The workers searched the jungle for wood that had straight trunks for the planks and natural bends for the ribs. They tore them off the drowned wreck because they didn't have nails. When those were exhausted, Cummins chiselled new fasteners out of wood. Canvas turned into a sail. Wax turned into caulk. Scavenged line strands were twisted into ropes.

Many of them were too blind from scurvy to walk without stumbling, and they worked in rags with blistering hands and straw hair. Bulkeley stated, "They are in so much pain that they can hardly see to walk." However, the boat that would save them was beginning to take shape, and they kept all of their remaining strength in its hull.

The air was torn one day by a shriek of panic. A rogue wave clawed at the partially constructed structure as it raced up the beach. The men charged into the water, dropping everything. Just ahead of the sea's raging clutches, they grabbed the skeleton of their dream and pulled it further inland. Then, trembling and soaked, they went back to work.

However, something else had started to stir in Captain Cheap.

In solitude he combed his maps, charting a course through the waters to the south. He estimated that Chiloé, a Spanish colony 350 miles north of the island, was located. They could not only endure but also attack if they could get there—by ark, cutter, barge, and yawl.

Cheap no longer saw it as an escape. It had to do with atonement.

He would assault a Spanish merchant ship, take its provisions and supplies, and then set out to reunite with Commodore Anson. They would then carry on with their mission, possibly even capturing the legendary galleon. The idea of winning, of coming back as a naval hero rather than a disgraced castaway, consumed him like a fire.

For now, he kept the plan to himself. It would be necessary to persuade the men. But with the zeal of the doomed, he believed it.

He would later remark, "We need not be afraid to accept prizes." "The Commodore might still be here."

A crippled fleet, a rebellious crew, and a bloodstained captain so constructed an ark—not of mercy, but of ambition—on a desolate island distant from any compass rose. Not just of wood, but of insanity, despair, and a final attempt to create the appearance of grandeur.

Following Cozens's funeral, the island appeared to be calmer, but behind the calm, a storm was building—one of will rather than weather. It culminated on July 30 when Bulkeley discovered young Byron by himself in his hut as he neared the outskirts of the improvised community. The youngster was bent over a worn volume—Sir John Narborough's chronicles—his eyes half-starved but yet alight with the ancient flame of seafaring romance. He was noble by birth but had now been beaten by misery.

Bulkeley requested to borrow the book for strategic purposes rather than for leisure reading. They now lived in the rocky southern areas Narborough had previously sailed through. Once considered a curiosity, his journal had turned into a lifeline. A possible route off the infamous Wager Island was hidden among its sea-stained pages.

Ever obedient, Byron consented to lend it—but only after getting Captain Cheap's approval. After all, the book was his. After he was in his quarters, Bulkeley read it more intently and with the same respect he showed The Christian's Pattern. An alternative to the lethal Drake Passage, Narborough's thorough notes on the Strait of Magellan depicted a terrifying but manageable passage through the southern tip of South America. Bulkeley thought the men could break through the strait, escape the Pacific, and drift north to Brazil if they could finish their ark and gather the three smaller boats. That war-neutral country might still provide safe refuge.

In any case, it was a crazy concept. They were separated from salvation by a perilous sea that was about 3,000 kilometers long. The strait itself was a winding maze of rocky traps and shoals, blanketed in fog and buffeted by erratic storms. "A man may mistake the right channel, and steer in among the broken islands and rocks, so far as to endanger his ship," Narborough had cautioned bluntly. But it was the only way forward for Bulkeley.

He justified what some could consider mutiny by writing, "Desperate diseases demand desperate remedies." It was suicide, the Drake Passage. The only options available in the Pacific, with its Spanish guards, were jail or death. Their greatest option was the Strait of Magellan, which was hardly feasible. Along the way, Narborough had even recorded the presence of food, including penguins, birds, and mussels.

But Bulkeley's thoughts went beyond navigation. This was a liberating course. It meant turning down the inept leadership of a captain who had lost his ship and his mind. It meant taking agency back from a Navy that had let them down. It meant surviving according to their own rules.

Bulkeley came to the conclusion that "our longboat can be fit for no enterprise but the preservation of life."

He met with the other navigators and Master Clark. They agreed after studying Narborough's itinerary and tracing it on the crude maps. Bulkeley then presented the men with the proposal while they stood at a somber fork in the road. Disobey Cheap and head east, homeward, or follow him north and risk conflict with a Spanish armada.

Cheap, however, had his own narrative and his own scheme. They would complete the assignment, he had declared, his voice still tinted with power. They would find Commodore Anson, head north, and return to the main campaign. He asserted that redemption and glory yet awaited. Byron adored sea stories that promised honor to those who persevered, and Cheap's remarks reflected those tales. However, those assurances were not new to the men. They had interred them next to Cozens in the muck.

Once bound together by the ark's promise, the outpost broke apart like the hull of the Wager. On one side: Cheap, with a shrinking number of followers supporting him, his hold growing tighter. Bulkeley and his expanding legion, on the other hand, were people who preferred to live rather than die for false hopes.

Byron was caught between two worlds. He was an aristocrat who had been up with a strong sense of honor and order, and he had long viewed Cheap as a tragic hero—a man who was holding onto his dignity while everything else was falling away. However, Bulkeley was clever and pragmatic, having demonstrated his worth by deeds rather than prestige. Leadership was not something he inherited. It was his creation.

Byron found it difficult. With growing doubt smearing the ink of loyalty, he scribbled his thoughts cautiously. Cheap had become unpredictable, desperate to hold onto power by force. Bulkeley stated, "The loss of the ship was the loss of him." Command was law at sea. Cheap's law had no anchor on land.

The pivotal moment was approaching on August 3. Byron learned that Bulkeley had summoned a council. The majority of the men would go. They would talk about what to do next. They would decide. A line is drawn.

Should Byron remain with the captain—follow custom, submit to authority, and risk destruction for the sake of duty? Should he join the men, defy orders, support survival, and risk being labeled a traitor?

The wind rustled the branches outside his hut like ghosts whispering.

The pages of Narborough's book were in the hand of the boy who had once dreamed of ships and stars.

There was more to the journey ahead.

It was rebellion. as well as history.

As if to foretell the weight of what lay ahead, the sky pressed low on the marooned outpost on the morning of July 31st, breaking gray and heavy. With the damp dirt still sticking to his boots, Captain Cheap was standing just outside his house when he noticed Bulkeley coming slowly toward him—and he wasn't the only one. There was a line of men behind him, some stiff-backed with resolution, others hollow-eyed and slumped from hunger. Together, they resembled a jury meeting on the rough edge of the globe rather than in a courthouse.

Bulkeley stopped a few steps away and pulled a piece of parchment, smeared, folded, and wet with perspiration and salt. A petition was made. He started reading out loud with the formality of a parliamentary clerk:

"After careful consideration, we, whose names are listed below, believe that the best, safest, and most effective method for preserving the bodies of people on the spot is to proceed across the Strait of Magellan for England."

Performed on a barren island off the coast of Patagonia.

Although the remark was delivered with tactful diplomacy, it made it quite evident that the soldiers were selecting a new commander and a new destiny.

With tremors in his fingertips, Cheap examined the names on the paper Bulkeley handed him. The aged cook Maclean, the seaman John Duck, Master Clark, and Pemberton, the head of the marines, all jumped out of the page one after the other. Midshipman Campbell, his enforcer, had signed as well. And at the bottom, Byron—young, impressionable Byron—had scrawled his name, if grudgingly.

It was a lengthy list. Too much time. There was no realistic method to discipline his crew because so many of them had disobeyed him. They were not a business anymore. They rebelled.

Cheap, however, noted who had not signed. Harvey, the purser. Elliot the surgeon. Hamilton, the Marine Lieutenant. Plastow, the steward. Above all, his second in command, Lieutenant Baynes, had remained faithful. The naval command structure was still in place, albeit tenuously.

With a harsh voice, Cheap dismissed the delegation, promising to review the petition and provide a response when it was ready. Not only did he need time to consider the strategy, but he also needed time to find out how to keep his command from falling apart.

Bulkeley and Cummins were called to Cheap's cabin two days later. The summons was a dramatic display of authority. Lieutenant Baynes, austere and solemn, sat inside next to him like a sign of formal order.

Cheap didn't waste any time.

"This paper has caused me a lot of anxiety—so much so that I haven't gone to sleep until eight this morning, just to think about it," he said, pointing to the petition.

He asserted that the signatories were unaware of the actual risks associated with their strategy. He contended that the trip to Brazil was much longer than the one to Chiloé and that they would be sailing against the wind all the time with little water and no guarantee of resupply. He claimed that their illusion of a simple escape was based on deceptive assurances.

Calmly but forcefully, Bulkeley retorted. A month's supply of fresh water may be transported by the longboat. Foraging on land would be an option for the smaller craft. In a deliberate attempt to minimize the threat, he claimed that the strait only provided "Indians in canoes" rather than Spanish battleships.

Cheap remained unfazed. His tone became piercing.

He declared, "We can capture a trading ship in Chiloé."

Cummins's eyebrows went up. "And with what? We don't have any cannons."

Cheap retorted, "What are our muskets for, besides boarding an enemy ship?"

The hut's air grew heavier. Exasperated, Cummins retorted, "Sir, we are here because of you." Finally, the charge was made out loud. The Wager had been run aground by the skipper. They were doomed by the captain.

Cheap trembled in response, saying, "You don't know my directives. No commander has ever received any so severe before. He said that he had been obligated to go to the meeting place.

Bulkeley quickly attacked that reasoning. He asserted that a captain must constantly exercise prudence. Command needed discretion, whether it was given or not.

Cheap did not erupt, which was surprising. Rather, he provided a glimmer of hope: he might think about granting permission to travel east through the Strait of Magellan. He needed more time to make up his mind, though.

Bulkeley didn't believe it. He cautioned, "The people are uneasy." "Therefore, it is best to resolve as soon as possible."

Nevertheless, Baynes sat in silence, providing neither a lifeline nor an opinion.

Cheap's voice became strained as he shifted. "Are you able to raise any more objections?"

Bulkeley answered, "Yes, sir." "An additional one." He asked for a clear assurance that if they sailed together, Cheap would confer with his commanders before changing direction, mooring, or initiating any hostile action.

It was as if the room held its breath.

Cheap's face turned red. This was a challenge to the entire foundation of naval authority, not merely a request. His voice was hammering the air.

"Your commander is still me!"

Bulkeley did not flinch as he nodded. "As long as you have the right to rule, we will give you our lives in support."

With Cummins by his side, he turned and walked away. Cheap was sitting behind them, in the dim inside of a hut that was quickly turning into a tomb of command, holding the petition in one hand and the vanishing appearance of submission in the other.

By the end of August, Wager Island had changed from being a camp for castaways to a small battleground, a colony of enemies rather than survivors. Everything was changing around John Byron: authority, allegiances, even the ground beneath their feet.

Captain Cheap had transformed his cottage into a stronghold, still holding on to the final remnants of his disintegrating leadership. He was in charge of the store tent and could access the rest of the armory. The walls were lined with muskets. At his side, like silent threats, lay a pair of swords, honed to a vicious sheen. Always on the lookout, Lieutenant Hamilton now carried a knife at all times and followed Cheap like a wolf at his master's heels. They stood watch day and night, as though under siege.

However, Cheap was aware that he was outnumbered as well as outgunned by firearms. He sent the purser as an emissary to the seceders with words of alliance and flasks of brandy in a final effort to tip the scales. However, the offer was turned down. The rebel group was untamed, arrogant, and becoming more independent.

When Bulkeley learned of the bribe, he called it just that—bribery. He was not going to allow Cheap to win people over with alcohol. The gunman actually had his own militia coming together. He had started gathering weapons and scrounging from the shipwreck, just like Cheap. At night, his followers escaped, making their way through fog and debris to retrieve rusting muskets and powder kegs. Each weapon and bullet was a proclamation.

"Bulkeley and his men are all in a capacity of bidding their officers defiance," acknowledged Midshipman Campbell, who remained sympathetic to Cheap, confirming what many had come to fear.

Interaction between the opposing factions had degenerated into acrid quiet. They were miles away in faith, yet a musket's distance apart. Neither man would go straight to the other. Rather, like sovereign states on the verge of civil war, they exchanged petitions and threats through messengers—envoys from opposing courts.

Then, one morning, everyone was shocked by a message from Cheap. Through Lieutenant Baynes, he suggested that on the upcoming Sabbath, Bulkeley's spacious quarters—one of the few shelters that can accommodate a significant number of people—be utilized as a chapel. "All factions should come together and pray," Cheap stated. A holy truce.

At first glance, it appeared to be a sign of reconciliation, acknowledging that despite their plight, they were still subject to the laws of heaven.

Bulkeley, however, noticed something else. A trap.

In his diary, he wrote, "We think religion has the least share in this proposal." "We might be taken by surprise and have our arms taken away from us in the middle of our devotion in order to thwart our plans if our tent is transformed into a house of prayer."

He refused. The war also deepened its trench, despite the fact that it was still bloodless.

From his precarious position between the groups, Byron could see that the island itself was fracturing. The guys conducted secret councils among the trees, moved in shadows, and talked behind shelters. New concerns were sparked by treachery rumors. The marine leader who had switched to Bulkeley's side, Pemberton, started drilling his skeletal soldiers in plain daylight. The fog of the island was broken by the clack of musket fire. Barefoot and ragged, the seamen practiced firing, pointing, reloading, and forming lines.

Even during the War of Jenkins' Ear, Byron had never witnessed actual warfare in his brief career. He was now afraid that he would be facing his own crew members in his first combat experience.

Tensions deteriorated. Depleted of its resources, the island appeared poised to explode.

The earth then did just that on August 25.

A low, terrible groan rose from the earth, and Byron felt it before he heard it. Then everything started to shake. The earth under him trembled, branches moved violently in tandem, and the walls of his home rattled. He briefly believed that it had arrived—an assault, a cannon boom, the first wave of rebellion.

However, it was an older thing. deeper.

An earthquake.

Only an earthquake.

But in its unadulterated strength, it reflected what had been accumulating for weeks: a downward pressure where alliances shattered like tectonic plates and each soldier awaited the first shot to be fired—not by chance, but by one of his own.

------- * * * -------

Chapter 16
MY MUTINEERS

A quieter but no less destabilizing tremor started to build two days after the earthquake that rocked Wager Island—what John Bulkeley had called the "violent shocks and tremblings of the earth"—took place. Bulkeley called his closest associates to a secret meeting on August 27, just as the island appeared to be descending into a spooky silence. In a world where every word they spoke may endanger their lives, the men congregated in whispers and shadows.

Three weeks previously, Captain Cheap had been handed a petition, calling for a course for Brazil and a break from the fatal dream of rejoining Anson, to which he had yet to reply. The silence was sufficient response for Bulkeley. Cheap would never give in. Like a man chained to a sinking mast, he was bound to his initial commands. He'd die with his illusions unharmed.

Bulkeley spoke out loud at this meeting what had hitherto been unthinkable: mutiny.

This wasn't the sarcastic mutterings of an irate sailor or the minor disobedience of an inebriated crewman. This was the most extreme and dangerous kind of treason—a revolt from within the same system that was designed to put an end to it. The Royal Navy considered mutiny to be a cancer, not merely a crime, and those who committed it were condemned to death. They were still remembering Cozens's destiny. They too could be shot and buried in the mud without a ceremony if they make one mistake.

Bulkeley countered that they had no other option. He asserted that castaways were exempt from the Navy's code. He asserted that the Navy's regulations are insufficient to guide us. They were in a natural state, out of Whitehall's and Portsmouth's grasp. Sovereignty in this place belonged to those who could protect life, not hold onto antiquated power.

In a stunning rhetorical shift, he portrayed Cheap as the real mutineer—the guy who had broken the Navy's basic essence by shooting a subordinate, defying advice, and ignoring reason—rather than the legitimate captain.

Bulkeley, however, was no idiot. He was aware that they would require a defense, one that would stand up in a court-martial in the future. Every action had to be recorded, every reason kept safe. He had been diligently recording every incidence that demonstrated Cheap's incapacity to lead in his journal. He now had to write for history as much as the present.

Lieutenant Baynes would be the key to their strategy. Their insurrection would appear as a reordering of command for survival rather than a takeover of power if Baynes, the next-highest ranking naval commander, were to take nominal charge. In private, Baynes had said that he thought the Brazil proposal made sense. However, he was hesitant since he didn't want to be on the losing side of a civil war. Ultimately, Adam Baynes, his grandfather, had previously supported Cromwell's Parliamentarians. He was thrown into the Tower of London at the return of the monarchs.

Bulkeley persisted, though. The whole framework of their defense would remain intact if Baynes would simply accept the title of commander. The lieutenant finally consented, but only after offering Cheap one last opportunity to sign an official declaration recognizing the shift in direction. He may continue to serve as captain in name if he consented, but his authority would be severely curtailed.

Bulkeley wrote, "We believe him to be a gentleman deserving of a limited command." "However, he is too dangerous to be trusted with an absolute one."

Bulkeley wrote the remarks down on a piece of paper that night. It was cautious, bordering on legalistic. The corporation was "plagued by robberies and internecine feuds," it said, and the only way to keep things in order was to cross the Strait of Magellan back to England. This was the last offer. Cheap would lose the captaincy if he didn't agree.

The plan was put into action the following morning.

A group of armed men commanded by Bulkeley and Baynes arrived to Cheap's house. Armed with pistols and muskets, they were prepared for any opposition. Cheap sat inside with his remaining armed loyalists at his sides. No shots were fired during the standoff.

Bulkeley read the petition out loud after unfolding it. In the little space, the words weighed heavily. He held out the paper after he was done. "Sir, will you sign it?"

Cheap's eyes were blazing with rage. He didn't think twice.

"No," he yelled. "You've denigrated my honor."

No discussion or pause for rationalization was place. Just fury.

The delegation turned and walked away. They marched straight to the marine commander Pemberton's hut. The crowd was already starting to form there. Rumors about the altercation had spread among cooks, marines, and seamen. In front of them, Bulkeley declared the truth: Cheap had rejected the plan, rejected peace, and rejected them.

Resolved, Pemberton stood and swore allegiance, saying, "I will stand by the people with my life." "For England!" echoed from every corner of the tent.

Finally, Cheap came out of his house. The audience became quiet.

"What's all the fuss about?" he insisted.

Bulkeley and his officers moved forward. "The men have decided to give Lieutenant Baynes command, sir."

Like a cannon shot into fog, Cheap's words echoed. "Who will take over the command from me?" He fixed Baynes with his gaze. "Is that you?"

The world appeared to be still. The lieutenant was looked at by everybody. It was time to make a choice.

Baynes turned pale. The color faded from his face.

He said the scarcely audible words, "No, sir." "It's not me."

And the whole strategy fell apart in that moment. Terrified, Baynes had given up on the cause. He had opted for quiet over disobedience. loyalty as opposed to freedom. Or maybe—living through everything.

There was no figurehead left for the mutineers. They couldn't claim legitimacy without Baynes. Like the earthquake before it, the revolt had trembled—and broken—as the wind howled all around them.

Captain David Cheap sat alone himself in his armed bunker in the days after the attempted coup, surrounded by his memories of power and his depleting arsenal of weaponry. The castaways' voices became bolder and louder outside. He heard them drilling once more, marching in formation, shouting orders, and shooting into the wind with their repurposed muskets. However, he could no longer command his wind. Cheap could feel the weight of the island crushing against his hut's walls as it had turned.

His world was falling apart—not with a yell of mutiny, but with the steady, methodical sound of footfall.

Harvey, the purser, had abandoned him and moved stealthily to Bulkeley's side. But something more profound was shattered by the news of his steward, Peter Plastow. From their very first days together, Plastow had been his dedicated servant. What remained if even he had defected?

Cheap, holding on to incredulity, called him. "Is that accurate?" he inquired.

Plastow remained unflinching. "Yes, sir. I want to travel to England, therefore I'll take a chance.

He was labeled a villain by Cheap. Then he denounced them all, villains and rebels alike, his voice rising in rage. Plastow was dismissed by him, and he departed silently, carrying the final remnant of allegiance with him.

Technically still in command, the captain sat in his bunker surrounded by swords and muskets, almost alone, only because no one had yet the audacity to forcibly remove him. He was aware of Bulkeley's handcuffs. In England, the gunner might be hanged and labeled a traitor if Baynes didn't formally back him. Without legal protection, mutiny was suicide.

Then Cheap did something nobody saw coming.

He told Bulkeley to come talk to him. By themselves.

Bulkeley accepted the invitation, even if it smacked of danger. Despite having guards with him, he went alone into Cheap's hut with a loaded pistol in his belt. A cocked pistol rested on Cheap's leg as he sat on his sea chest within.

Two men who had formerly performed the same mission, now enemies on a desolate, godforsaken island, locked eyes. Bulkeley lifted his weapon slowly. Cheap remained motionless, saying nothing. After hesitating, Bulkeley started to retreat gradually.

He would later remark that he did not want to be "compelled to discharge a pistol at a gentleman for my own preservation."

The men waited outside.

Then, however, an extraordinary event occurred.

Cheap came out, unarmed.

With scores of individuals watching him, the environment was tense as he entered the commotion. The same mob that had plotted against him was now quiet. Bulkeley subsequently acknowledged, "Here the Captain displayed all the conduct and courage imaginable." Not a single one of his adversaries dared to raise a hand as he stood alone. Bulkeley, no. Not Pemberton. Not even the bruised boatswain King.

For a brief time, authority had returned—not by coercion, but simply being there.

Time was running out, though. They were being killed by the island itself.

Men dropped all around John Byron, and he stared helplessly. In an attempt to delay the inevitable, Byron heartbreakingly gave him the last of his dried mussels, piece by piece, after one collapsed next to him. However, it was insufficient.

Nevertheless, he passed away.

Fifty were dead already. Others mumbled the unimaginable, hungry beyond recognition. The corpse had been chopped before it was buried by a hungry boy. Others did what no man wanted to record, and they did it in secrecy. It was dubbed the "last extremity" by Byron.

They had to get out. Or death, or what death made them become, would devour them all up.

After being marooned for 144 days, Byron finally glanced out and blinked on October 5. He initially believed it to be an illusion brought on by hunger. However, it was genuine.

The ark was finished.

There was now a completed hull where there had been strewn boards and fantasies. The new longboat, fifty feet long and ten feet broad, loomed out of its blocks like a mythical ship. They had installed a bowsprit, a tiller, a deck, and a hold. Food and powder storage space below. There's room for hope above.

To seal the hull, they applied tallow and wax. However, how can such a large ship be launched?

They came up with a solution because they were too weak to haul it: a wooden track of logs that rolled below the boat like chariot wheels. The longboat dragged toward the sea, groaning slowly.

After tying the rope and raising the masts, they gave her the name Speedwell, which comes from an old buccaneer legend in which a stranded crew had done the same and survived.

Bulkeley declared that God had saved them while observing her bob in the tide.

Byron cried in private. He missed the comforts of letters and linen, his sister Isabella, and England. Even the notoriously vicious "Wicked Lord," his brother, didn't seem so horrible anymore.

However, Byron also had a final delusion: perhaps, just possibly, they could all go together. That the sea might take them home, not simply to England, but to forgiveness, leaving the resentment and betrayal on the island.

It was the hope of a boy. However, it blazed more brilliantly than any fire they had started since the accident.

On October 9, 1741, a group of wandering ghosts emerged from their hiding places and started to congregate in the pale dawn. Bone hung from their flesh. They were dressed in tatters. Their hope was bleached out by cold and malnutrition, and their eyes had gone distant. However, they carried bayonets, pistols, and muskets—whatever was left of the iron teeth of war—in their hands. At the front of the march, John Bulkeley, who was now more of a warlord than a gunner, distributed weapons and gave orders.

It was no longer a matter of law or loyalty. It was a matter of survival. Additionally, former captain and current captor David Cheap stood in their way.

The rebels crossed the ruins of what had been a royal outpost in silence, bayonets loaded and hammers cocked. The sea groaned beside them. Overhead, Mount Misery loomed. And they arrived at Cheap's bunker in the fading half-light.

They threw open the door.

Cheap, skinny and hollowed out by misery, had been sleeping on the ground. His own guys were rushing at him when he woke up. It was too late when he reached for his revolver. They restrained him. Later, an officer called it "somewhat rude." Some were not as understanding. Cheap's final devoted sword, Lieutenant Hamilton, was taken in a nearby hut in a coordinated attack.

There would be no turning back this time. Lieutenant Baynes had joined the uprising as well.

After giving them a disbelieving look, Cheap spoke gravely in shock, "Gentlemen, do you know what you have done?"

Bulkeley's response was stern and icy: he was being arrested for Cozens' murder.

"I remain your commander," Cheap said. He took the letter from Commodore Anson—the one that made him captain of His Majesty's Ship Wager—from his chest. He extended it like a cross. "Take a look. Take a look! I couldn't have imagined that you would treat me that way.

Bulkeley said, "You are to blame, sir." "You have shown no concern for the welfare of the public."

Cheap turned away from the authorities and spoke to the sailors who were observing. You have caught me dozing off, gentlemen. My policemen are scoundrels, but you are a bunch of courageous people.

"My lads, I do not blame you," he said, bound now, his wrists behind his back. That is my officers' villainy.

He then faced Baynes.

"All right, sir. What do you want me to do?"

Once standing on the brink of mutiny, Baynes now stood squarely within it. Cheap would have to stay in a tent, he retorted. Half-dressed but still wearing his hat, the captain pleaded to stay in his own.

"Refused," Baynes stated.

Cheap sneered, defiant, and bitter. Captain Baynes, all right!

Following his captors, he ventured outside into the icy cold. The crowd dispersed. His back was stiff, but his hands were bound.

He remarked icily, "I apologize for not taking off my hat; my hands are confined."

Even Bulkeley, who documented Cheap's demise, observed the odd nobility at the time. Cheap had lost—but in that moment, surrounded by adversaries and humiliation, he was finally calm. Finally, a captain.

Then, suddenly, King, the boatswain, who had been a faithful enforcer but was now furious, came up and hit Cheap in the face.

"Your time came," King growled. "But now it's mine, God damn you!"

Cheap remained unflinching. He glared and spat blood.

"You are a scoundrel for making a man sick while he is incarcerated."

He was under continual guard, as was Hamilton. Their prison was a makeshift shack, but they were always on guard—every visitor was searched, and there were six seamen and an officer on duty. Bulkeley didn't want to take chances. He now had to govern the island that he had conquered.

Now that Cheap was neutralized, Bulkeley took over. "We now looked on him as Captain," said Midshipman Campbell, who remained devoted to the commander in spirit.

The last preparations for the trip to Brazil started. Rainwater was now placed inside barrels that had previously held powder. What little flour remained was loaded onto the Speedwell in bags. Bulkeley placed his notebook and The Christian's Pattern, his two most prized belongings, in the hold.

Still in disbelief, Byron expressed concern out loud that there wouldn't be enough food for a week. He wrote, "A mixture of seaweed was to lengthen out our flour."

Bulkeley created a new code of behavior in order to keep the island's instability from spilling over into the water. It was a desperate attempt to draft a constitution. It said:

All collected food and supplies will be split equally.

Regardless of station, a thieving man will be abandoned on the closest coast.

Any individual who threatens or uses violence against another will be left behind.

An oath, not etched in blood but in the collective understanding that without order, none would survive, had to be signed by every man who wanted to join the Speedwell.

The last question then arose.

How Should Cheap Be Handled?

On Wager Island, ninety-one persons were still alive, barely. The boats were packed. At sea, there was no cell. Caged among them, Cheap would be a continual threat. Bulkeley was aware of it. Everyone was aware of it.

Cheap, nevertheless, had one final move to make.

He requested to be abandoned.

He declared, "I'd rather be shot than taken away as a prisoner."

The crew weighed it and talked about it. At last, someone expressed what many were considering:

"Leave him alone and damn him."

Bulkeley then sat together with his officers and wrote a final document, this time for the Admiralty. It was methodical, thorough, and devastating.

According to their writing, Cheap could not be carried "in so small a vessel, and for so long and tedious a passage."

It would be disastrous to take him.

They decided to leave their commander behind in order to "avoid murder."

With his boots buried in the wet sand of what history would refer to as Cheap's Bay, Captain David Cheap stood at the edge of the island, alone yet unflinching. A collapsing outpost behind him. The water in front of him. And treachery behind his back.

He had escaped death's ghostly jaws, insubordination, madness, and starvation. He was now confronted with his worst punishment to date: desertion.

It was obvious to Cheap. Cozens' shot served as a smokescreen for the men. Their deliberate efforts to silence him were reflected in their mutiny, rebellion, and well-crafted pronouncements. since they were aware of the reality. And they were aware that they might end up on the gallows rather than in glory if Cheap ever made it to England and shared his account of events.

Thus, they provided him with a boat. Or, more accurately, what could have been.

The 18-foot wreck of a yawl had just been dashed into the rocks. Like a shattered animal, its ribs were visible through the break in its shell. As if explaining his own state, Cheap mumbled, "All in pieces." They left him with this deathtrap, a Bible, two broken rifles, a rusted telescope, some salted meat that smelt of decay, a few handfuls of rancid flour, and a compass that swayed as though it didn't know what true north was.

He took them all. Nothing more could be taken.

Cheap's final circle had now diminished to a mere glimmer. Both Lieutenant Hamilton and the surgeon, Elliot, remained faithful to him until the very end. However, Byron, Campbell, and the others had escaped. Once radical in their resistance, even the seceders had lost their zeal. The majority were only remaining because they had nowhere else to go. Mitchell and two other people had already attempted to flee; they had rigged a homemade raft and disappeared into the surf, never to be seen again.

Cheap was one of ten men still on the island. Ten guys to confront the cold, the wind, and the repercussions.

Bulkeley's group was ready to leave on October 14, 1741, more than a year after they had sailed from England with aspirations of conquest, and five arduous months after the Wager had split apart on the rocks. Brazil was their destination, followed by home. Or what would remain of it.

The vessels were crammed as full as coffins. The Speedwell was packed with fifty-nine soldiers. They crammed twelve into the cutter. The barge has ten. Bulkeley remarked that even the toughest prison in England "is a palace to our present situation."

By now they were half-men, frightened, starving into silence, and barely dressed. The boats, however, were able to float. And it was sufficient.

Cheap was present to bid them farewell. After being freed from captivity, he walked to the beach beneath a bruised sky and observed the men passing him one by one. He had formerly mentored Midshipman Byron, who was present. Master Clark and his kid, the angry boatswain King, the aged cook Maclean, the purser Harvey, the young Isaac Morris, and the seamen John Duck and John Jones were all present. There was a recollection of tension, of friendship, or of silent resistance in every face that went by him.

As they got on board, several yelled taunts.

One exclaimed, "You'll never see an Englishman again."

"I hope the island is a good fit for you!" said another.

Cheap remained silent.

Bulkeley himself then came over.

Old command and new, captain and gunner, their eyes met. Cheap, unshaven and with lifeless eyes, held out his hand.

"I hope your journey is safe," he remarked.

Bulkeley paused, then accepted it.

Later, with a hint of remorse, he would write in his journal, "This was the last time I ever saw the unfortunate Captain Cheap."

At eleven, the sails were raised. The waves broke. With oars slapping against the sea, the boats struggled and suddenly broke free from the land. Bulkeley led them out of the cove from the Speedwell's commander's position.

Cheap's Bay closed in their wake.

Cheap stood silently on the shore, his eyes shaded by his hat.

He had begged Bulkeley to recount the whole story if they made it to England. His tale.

That pledge was never fulfilled.

A final fact weighed heavily on Cheap as the sails disappeared over the horizon. He might not only pass away on that island, but his account might remain there forever.

He looked at the yawl's damaged hull, the sky that was battered, and the sea that had sucked in so many. Captain David Cheap vanished from history in that quiet, his voice all but forgotten.

The court-martial, that is.

Until the truth finally surfaced.

------- * * * -------

Part Four
Deliverance

Chapter 17

BYRON'S CHOICE

The sea was dark and unsettled beneath a blanket of cloud as the boats departed from the shore. John Byron remained at the stern, his gaze riveted on a spectral figure that shrank in the mist—Captain Cheap, marooned and motionless, a broken silhouette against the shore. Byron had anticipated that the captain, despite being deposed, would be brought aboard at least as a prisoner. However, the vessels had abandoned him. No sail, no sustenance, and not even a functional vessel. A mere sliver of beach and the unsettling realization that his men had abandoned him to perish. The words were heavy with regret as Byron later confessed in his journal, "I had all along been in the dark as to the turn this affair would take."

Byron had initially reconciled himself to the idea of returning. He was of the opinion that abandoning the mission could potentially save his life, even if it resulted in the termination of his career. However, this—this felt distinct. No matter how defective, this was a betrayal by a commander. Byron's interior narrative—the romantic self-image he had cultivated amidst the chaos—began to crumble as Cheap grew smaller and the fog gradually closed around him. Some men shouted three half-hearted cheers for their former captain, but the sound scarcely reached the shore. And then he vanished.

It was only a matter of minutes before the sea suddenly turned on them. A sudden squall struck with a ferocity that appeared to be almost divine. The longboat's makeshift foresail had split, causing it to flail uncontrollably and snap like a whip. Byron heard a sharp fracture. The vessels were compelled to retreat and sought refuge in a nearby lagoon, which was no more than a mile from the island from which they had just fled.

Bulkeley requested that volunteers return to Wager Island the following day to retrieve a canvas tent that had been abandoned, while the men were repairing the sail. Although it was a trivial task, it was a significant occasion for Byron. He and Midshipman Campbell expressed their willingness to depart, and as they navigated the chop, their voices were muffled by the salt and precipitation. The actions they had taken and the involvement they had had were improper. Although Cheap may have been cruel, abandoning him to his death was an entirely different form of barbarism. Now was the moment for them to reclaim their honor, if they ever aspired to do so.

The abandonment had also caused concern for other individuals aboard the barge, including Cheap's former companions. They contributed their voices to the counterplot out of concern that they would be executed for mutiny if they returned to England. They would unite to reclaim their commander.

Byron, rowing with a subdued intensity, began to contemplate whether Bulkeley would suspect their strategy. Would he pursue them for the theft of the barge? They were aware that Bulkeley could not afford to lose it, as it was one of the few vessels that could transport hunting parties to the shore. The returning party observed a faint flicker as dusk fell, as if campfires were dancing in the mist like will-o'-the-wisps. They returned to their residence. Returning to Wager Island.

Their return left Cheap, emaciated, and disoriented. Upon learning of their mission, his countenance was illuminated with a sense of optimism that had not been witnessed in weeks. Byron, Campbell, the surgeon Elliot, and Lieutenant Hamilton convened in Cheap's temporary shelter that evening to exchange plans, stories, and potentialities. For the first time in weeks, there was camaraderie that was not derived from desperation, but rather from choice.

However, hunger was not eradicated by faith.

The following morning, Byron was confronted with a stark reality. He possessed only the last strands of a waistcoat, shredded trousers, and a tattered hat. His stomach was vacant, and his feet were bare. The others were not significantly superior. Bulkeley's crew had retained their food rations. The meat that Cheap provided was half-rotten and covered in decomposition. Byron concluded that in order to endure, they would have to reclaim their legitimate portion of the provisions.

Cheap cautioned against it. "They will seize the barge," he declared. "Upon your return, you will discover that we have vanished."

However, Byron had conducted a thorough analysis. The vessel would be concealed. He and Campbell would proceed on foot, following the coastline. Indeed, it would be perilous. However, starvation was a form of insanity in its own right.

Their feet were torn and raw as they set out again the following morning, rowing to another shore and then trekking inland through swamp and thorny vegetation. They reached the lagoon's edge as night descended. As usual, Bulkeley's soldiers were scavenging for food, as evidenced by the echoing of voices. The mutineers' perplexity was transformed into tension upon observing the two midshipmen.

"Where is the barge?" Bulkeley demanded.

Byron maintained his composure. "We will not abandon Captain Cheap," he declared, his voice resembling a blade.

Bulkeley's expression was distorted. He was unable to comprehend this reversal. He later ascribed it to Byron's aristocratic pride in his journal, writing bitterly that the "Honourable Mr. Byron" could not tolerate living among common sailors.

Bulkeley and Baynes became belligerent when the midshipmen requested their food rations. One of them spat, "You're a jerk." "Return the barge, or you will receive nothing."

Byron directly appealed to the males. He was greeted with icy glances. "Bring the boat," they requested. "Alternatively, we will arrive with weapons and seize it ourselves."

Byron's heart thudded as he turned away. But then, a sudden gust of wind snatched his headwear and hurled it into the darkness. Seaman John Duck, an old friend, slowly approached, removed his own hat, and placed it in Byron's hands.

"I am grateful, John," Byron murmured, his voice choked with emotion. However, he was unable to endure it. He returned it and continued to walk.

Under the cover of darkness, Byron and Campbell returned to the concealed barge. In silence, they rowed across the black water, casting cautious glimpses over their shoulders for any indication of a cutter, whose cannon mouth gleamed in the darkness.

Their reputation remained unblemished. Their survival is dubious.

However, they had elected to demonstrate fortitude. In the shadows of Wager Island, that decision would determine the legacy of all those who persisted.

------- * * * -------

Chapter 18
PORT OF GOD'S MERCY

Bulkeley issued the directive shortly after the wind had abated. With Lieutenant Baynes by his side and two fragile vessels beneath them, they permanently abandoned Wager Island. Bulkeley declined to return, despite the fact that the outpost where Captain Cheap and the others were stationed was within reach. No confrontation, no assault. The vessel was abandoned. He opted for the open sea and the southward draw of the Strait of Magellan, manifesting finality in his silence and resolve in his departure. There would be no more contemplation of the past.

The subsequent events were not merely a journey. It was a furnace.

The Speedwell, initially a modest longboat, was now burdened by the impossibility of accommodating fifty-nine individuals. Their bodies were crammed together like tangled rigging, with their appendages wedged between barrels, masts, and broken planks. She was not designed for this. Her decks, which were previously unobstructed, were now obstructed by casks of drinking water and crates of ammunition intended to repel fictitious adversaries. Men were poised on every available surface, including the tiller, the bow, and the dank darkness beneath the decks. Nowhere to slumber was available. There is no location to relieve oneself. No longer exists any sense of decorum.

They leaned over the edge of the hull to relieve themselves. Bulkeley was unable to compose due to the nausea caused by the odor of their soaked garments, which festered. He wrote, "The air we breathe is so noxious that it would be impossible for a man to live."

The accompanying vessel, a twenty-five-foot cutter, experienced a more severe fate. The dozen men aboard, including Purser Thomas Harvey, were huddled together like sacks on splintered benches, rising and falling with each surge, as they lacked both a hold and shelter. They sought refuge on the Speedwell during tempestuous nights, securing their vessel behind it. The main boat groaned under the weight of seventy-one desperate men on such evenings.

The vessels in question were not mere watercraft. They were floating prisons, coffins devoid of stakes. The males on board were already ghosts. Many were too frail to be concerned with their own survival or demise. Bulkeley grimly observed, "They truly seem to be indifferent." Nevertheless, he persevered, serving as captain in all but name. A dynamic that festered beneath every command Bulkeley gave was that Baynes, by technical rank, still held authority.

Another squall struck them on October 30, two weeks into this horror. Bulkeley observed a narrow and perilous channel along the mountainous coast as the sea heaved and twisted. This channel was enclosed by the same type of rocks that had ripped open the Wager. His gaze shifted to Baynes. Cummins had confidence in the carpenter. He made the decision: they would be thrown into the boulders. He wrote, "Keep the sea, and we shall see nothing but death." "And the same opportunity to engage in land speculation."

They navigated the pandemonium with the help of shouted commands, half-prayers, and raw instinct. Breakers resounded with the force of cannon discharge. They would crumble with a single error. However, the boats miraculously navigated between the rocks and entered a concealed cove, where the cliffs rose like cathedral walls and cascades cascaded down the crystalline flanks. Bulkeley, his vanity briefly swollen, asserted that the entire British Navy could anchor in such a location.

However, they did not remain for an extended period.

The cutter was dispatched to collect fresh water and any crustaceans that Providence might provide. Then they sailed once more, plunging headlong into the rumbling of the southern ocean.

The cutter's mainsail ruptured on November 3, as the decks were battered by torrents of rain and the crew sought comfort by curling in on themselves. A few moments later, the vessel disappeared from view. Bulkeley repeatedly examined the surges from the Speedwell as it crested; however, the small boat and its crew were vanished—twelve men were absorbed whole. Among the victims were Harvey the purser, Richard Phipps, a cunning raft-builder, and William Oram, a carpenter's companion whom Bulkeley had personally persuaded to flee the seceders. Presently, all have disappeared.

Their minds were emptied by hunger and grief as they drifted into a coastal inlet to escape the escalating tempest. In the absence of the cutter, it was impossible to reach the shore in search of sustenance. Only a small number of individuals were capable of swimming. According to Bulkeley, "We are currently in an extremely distressing state." The remarks were a source of despair.

They made another attempt to depart on November 5, but the tempest repelled them like a gatekeeper from hell. They gazed wistfully at a cluster of mussels that were clinging to distant rocks, as they were wet and starving. The boatswain, King, subsequently constructed a grotesque raft from kegs and oars, which he secured with rope. Mounting it was accomplished by him and two others. They were propelled into the air by a wave. Two individuals were rescued. King kicked his way to the shore and returned with a modest cache of food—and a mystery.

King had discovered an empty cask on the shore. It was identified by the Royal Navy's insignia. The males became increasingly reticent. Had the Wager encountered the same fate as another British vessel, such as Anson's flagship Centurion?

They observed a white flash descending in the waves the following morning. The sail of the cutter. The twelve individuals who were missing had miraculously survived, despite being drenched to the bone and adrift for days. Bulkeley stated, "It imbued us with new life." However, it is only a transient respite.

The group reassembled in a cove. James Stewart remained behind, while the majority of the cutter's crew ascended the Speedwell to recover. The cutter was once again dispatched to collect shellfish.

The rope that connected the cutter to the Speedwell split at 2 a.m. in a tumult of wind and rain. Stewart drifted into the night in solitude. They summoned him. He never glanced back. He and the cutter were gone by morning, having collided with an unknown reef.

Despair intensified. They were unable to forage or access land in the absence of the cutter. On a single vessel, seventy individuals are currently crammed together like cattle. "The people were extremely uneasy," Bulkeley observed. "A significant number of them are in despair regarding a possible salvation."

The following day, eleven males approached with a frantic request: "Expel us." They would prefer to take their chances on land than to endure their demise at sea. Bulkeley and Baynes, aware of the legal implications, required the men to sign a declaration that they had voluntarily departed and that they were absolving their commanders of any responsibility.

The Speedwell approached the shore as closely as its keel permitted. The eleven individuals plunged into the frigid surf and proceeded to swim to a desolate island, never to be seen or heard from again in any British account. Their departure was definitive. Similar to spirits emerging from the deck and disappearing into the mist.

The Speedwell continued to sail.

No one could determine the direction. The sole difference is that it would conclude in the same manner as all ordeals: not in triumph, but in judgment. The journey would not be forgotten. A reckoning was imminent—not from the sea, but from the tribunals of men. Also, the trial would reveal the twisted anatomy of survival, in addition to the truth of the voyage.

November 10th. Bulkeley, who had been hunched over his journal for nearly a month since they had escaped the shattered remnants of Wager Island, elevated his eyes to a constellation of barren islands that stretched along the horizon. The air was unusually clear, and for the first time in days, there was a hint of geography, of names that had been engraved into naval lore for so long. He was of the opinion that they had reached the northwestern mouth of the Strait of Magellan, as indicated by his calculations and the severe, jagged silhouettes of the land.

He observed it to the south: a malevolent mass of black stone and serrated cliffs. Island of Desolation. The term itself—as characterized by Sir John Narborough as "so desolate a land to behold"—appeared to be more of a curse than a description. In this location, they were perched on the brink of the known universe.

However, these conditions were not conducive to triumph.

Bulkeley directed the Speedwell to head southeast in order to enter the strait and make the voyage he had envisioned, despite the storm and starvation. However, a wall of pandemonium rose to meet them as the prow turned. He confessed, "I have never seen a sea like this in my life," a sentiment that was distilled from a source that was more profound than mere pride. These were not insignificant surges. In a confrontation of gods, the Pacific and the Atlantic collided, as the waters fought for control. The winds raged with the intensity of a typhoon. The Speedwell, which was overburdened with gaunt men and saturated supplies, was unable to ride the waves. They consumed it.

Then, the surge arrived. At first, the deck inclined twenty degrees, then fifty, and finally eighty degrees. The boat sank, its sails flattening against the sea like a shroud, as it lay helplessly on its side. Bulkeley was certain that it was the conclusion. All of his calculations, his unyielding will, his defiance of Cheap, of mutiny, of the Crown itself—it would all be for naught. He would perish in the frigid waters that engulfed both empires and spirits, unidentified and in the cold.

However, the Speedwell rose. Gradually. Similar to a resurrection. The deck was flooded and water was emitted from the hold. The males, who were anticipating their imminent demise, were unable to comprehend their current state of existence.

And then, a grace of light—a cove, akin to a fissure between granite jaws. They accelerated the boat toward it, navigating through a series of breakers that were so close that, as Bulkeley put it, "a man could toss a biscuit on 'em." Nevertheless, they succeeded. The waters within were as tranquil as a millpond. Port of God's Mercy was the name provided by him for the refuge. "We regard our preservation today as a miracle," he wrote. Even the most resolute of them murmured promises of penance.

However, salvation was only transient.

The men's desperation and unruliness intensified with each passing day. Thinned rations. The skin was cinched around the bones. They pleaded for flour. Crumbs were the subject of their dispute. Bulkeley, Baynes, and Cummins endeavored to enforce the articles they had drafted weeks prior—rules for order and survival. Nevertheless, the males were no longer apprehensive about discipline. There was a greater dread of hunger among them. In the event that discipline was not enforced, Bulkeley, Baynes, and Cummins expressed their intention to abandon the ship. The men, cognizant of the fact that Bulkeley's cunning was their sole remaining compass, conceded. Presently.

Bulkeley dispersed a quantity of flour in order to quell the disturbance. There were numerous individuals who did not even prepare it. Their features were streaked with soot and salt, as they consumed it raw, akin to animals. Nevertheless, it was inadequate.

The youngest individual began to succumb to death.

George Bateman, who was sixteen years old, perished in silence after wasting away to a skeleton. The quiet finality of the utterly exhausted would be followed by others, who would collapse one by one. Bulkeley observed its progression. He stated that "numerous additional individuals must endure the same fate in the absence of prompt relief."

A twelve-year-old boy implored his shipmate for a small amount of extra wheat, sufficing to enable him to reach Brazil. A blank stare was the response to his supplication. Compassion had disappeared. Bulkeley stated, "Hunger is devoid of all compassion." Afterward, the boy passed away, his anguish brought to an end not by kindness, but by the cold mercy of death.

They entered a complex network of lagoons and channels by November 24, a labyrinth that even experienced mariners found perplexing. Bulkeley was accused by Baynes of leading them awry. Had they been traveling in circles for weeks, never truly crossing the strait?

Bulkeley was incensed. He responded, "We are currently in the Strait of Magellan, if there ever was such a place in the world." However, uncertainty had penetrated the crew's very core. They retraced their steps, exhausted.

Madness seeped in.

A thin, hysterical cackle that echoed off the cliffs elicited an uncontrollable chuckle from one marine. He collapsed and succumbed to his injuries. An additional one ensued. Their remains were immersed in the ocean without ceremony.

Two additional weeks have transpired. The sea, like an ancient riddle, disclosed the truth: they had been in the strait. Throughout the duration. They had squandered precious time and lives in a state of uncertainty and retreat. I am now heading eastward once more.

The most damning notion of all, perhaps, emerged in the silence that followed: It is possible that Cheap was correct. It is possible that they should have traveled to the north.

Their story would not conclude at this point, although it could have. Upon their eventual rescue, a portion of them would make it to England. Others would not. However, the sea, despite its ferocity, had not been the most severe arbiter.

That would occur at a later time.

Their deeds would be examined in the frigid theater of a military tribunal, in the candlelit corridors of the Admiralty. The dead lads, the cast-offs, the drowned, Bulkeley's rebellion, and Cheap's madness. A sinister truth would emerge amid those legal arguments and sworn testimonies—one about the brittleness of honor, the cost of obedience, and the extent to which a man will go when his world becomes a lifeboat.

------- * * * -------

Chapter 19
THE HAUNTING

Captain David Cheap was no longer the shattered man who had been marooned by mutiny by December. He had not renounced his mission, nor had he lost faith in his ability to reunite with Commodore Anson and the fragmented remnants of their squadron. Even those who had previously seceded now rallied to him, as desperation had a way of fostering unity. John Byron, Midshipman Campbell, Lieutenant Hamilton, and Surgeon Elliot comprised the remaining nineteen men. The men who were still stranded on Wager Island were hardened but not yet vanquished, as it had been two months since Bulkeley's party vanished across the sea.

They subsisted on seaweed and the occasional cormorant. The riotous mutinies and challenges to command were eliminated, and Cheap now commanded a more cooperative, hungry, and smaller group. A peculiar renewal ensued as a result of the adversity. Campbell noted that his pace had increased significantly. Cheap collected wood, ignited flames, and prepared whatever was feasible. He appeared to have been reincarnated as a result of necessity.

The men were able to restore the yawl to seaworthiness and fortify the battered barge by utilizing the skills they had recovered from their longboat repairs. Three containers of beef were miraculously recovered from the sunken Wager, and Cheap, foreseeing the situation, distributed the limited amount of edible beef. He would later write, "I then began to conceive great hopes."

A breach in the clouds on December 15 allowed sunlight to spread across the island. An portent was perceived by Cheap. He ascended Mount Misery with Byron and a few others and examined the horizon through his telescope. Their emotions were restless, despite the turbulent sea. The men were enthralled by ghost tales, including an apparition that was observed near the water, which the ghost of the murdered seaman James Mitchell had left unburied. Byron remembered a peculiar lament that bore a resemblance to drowning. Some individuals claimed to have observed a figure laboring in the surf by the light of the moon. Whether it was a hallucination or a haunting, it heightened their urgency to depart.

The barge, which was twenty-four feet in length, and the yawl, which was scarcely eighteen feet in length, were loaded. These were open vessels, lacking cabins and shelter, with only a crude mast and cross planks. The barge was occupied by Cheap, Byron, and eight other individuals. Campbell, Hamilton, and six additional individuals were transported aboard the yawl. The men were twisted around barrels, ropes, and one another, with scarcely a foot of space between them.

They departed from Wager Island at Cheap's signal. The wind-beaten remnants of their shelters sagged under the sky behind them, a monument to survival that the ocean would soon obliterate.

They were to traverse the Gulf of Pain for nearly 100 miles, followed by an additional 250 miles along the Pacific coast to Chiloé Island. It would be a test of will and physique.

Within the initial hour, the rain began to pummel them. The waves were flattened into avalanches as the wind blew out of the west. Cheap, who was always resourceful, instructed the men to form a human wall, with their backs against the sea and their arms locked, while they attempted to bail out the boats with their hands and caps. It was inadequate. The vessels were experiencing issues with foundering. Cheap issued the directive to discard the supplies as the vessel's hull was being torn apart by death. They observed the disappearance of food, water, and any other substance that could be lost into the sea. Hunger would occur at a later time. Drowning would occur immediately unless they took action.

They discovered a cove that evening and stumbled onto the shore. They attempted to locate refuge by ascending the damp cliffs, but their efforts were unsuccessful. They collapsed on a rock in the open, causing their bodies to freeze. Campbell wrote, "It froze so hard that by the morning, several of us were nearly dead." There was no place of refuge in this location. There is no timber available. There is no sustenance available. Nevertheless, Cheap redirected them to the vessels.

They continued to row with unwavering determination. They unfurled the patchwork sails and skimmed downwind when the wind shifted south. Seaweed, which they referred to as "sea-tangle," was consumed after it was peeled from boulders. Nine days have transpired. Almost one hundred miles were acquired.

Subsequently, a cape with three substantial cliffs was presented as a geographical gift. The conclusion of the Gulf. They were under the impression that the worst was behind them.

December 25th was the date.

They spent the night at the beach and celebrated Christmas with a feast of sea-tangle and stream water, which they referred to as "Adam's wine." King George II was honored with a toast by Cheap. Their toast was not celebratory; rather, it was defiant.

They approached the promontory a few days later. The ocean was in a state of turmoil. The waves ascended like mountains frosted in white, as currents roared between the boulders. Campbell referred to them as the "whitest of the whites." Sails that were purchased at a reduced cost were lowered. The males applied their full strength to the oars.

When they reached the initial cliff, they were compelled to retreat. They attempted to retreat to a nearby estuary, but they were unable to do so before nightfall due to their exhaustion. They slept on their oars. In the morning, their bodies were rigid and their hands were blistered, and they pursued their endeavors once more. This time, they reached the second precipice. Once more, the sea reprimanded them by propelling them rearward.

Still, the tempest continued to rage on the third morning. No one ventured to attempt the cape. Consequently, they proceeded to the shore in quest of sustenance. A seal was observed by a single individual. He elevated his musket and discharged it. Bones, fat, and skin were consumed after the flesh was roasted over a flame. The hide was employed by Byron to envelop his frostbitten ankles. There was no longer any waste. Life was lacking in substance.

The vessels were anchored just offshore that evening. On each vessel, two individuals were stationed as guards. The barge was where Byron's watch was located.

They had consumed food. They emanated tenderness. They harbored expectation.

As a result, they permitted themselves to slumber for the first time in weeks.

It is possible that they will traverse the final escarpment tomorrow.

It commenced with a resounding impact in the darkness.

Byron awoke to the sickening sound of the barge being flung like driftwood, with breakers roaring in every direction. The tempest had returned with ferocity, and it brought with it a sound that chilled him more than the waves: a shrieking. Not the weather, not the sea—something human. Something that is spectral. He turned in time to observe the yawl, which was anchored a short distance away, heave once, twice, and then vanish beneath a devastating wave.

Two males had been sleeping on board. One was thrown onto the stony beach by the tide, coughing and sputtering. The other never emerged.

The subsequent event was anticipated by Byron and his companion to be their own capsizing. Rowing fiercely to prevent a broadside impact, they hauled anchor and angled the barge into the waves, working against the sea's violence. The night stretched into an interminable, gray dawn.

Byron wrote, "We lay all the next day in a great sea, not knowing what would be our fate."

When they finally reunited on land, they were exhausted and soaked. The tally was bleak: only eighteen individuals remained. It was now impossible to transport all of them forward in the absence of the yawl. The vessel could accommodate a maximum of three additional passengers; any more would result in its sinking. Someone would have to be left behind.

The decision was made by Cheap with a cold tone in his voice. Smith, Hobbs, Hertford, and Crosslet were selected as marines. Soldiers, not mariners. At sea, a dead weight. Campbell documented, "This was a somber experience; however, we were compelled to do so by necessity." They provided the marines with a sauté pan, ammunition, and a musket. The remaining individuals ascended the vessel. The four men stood on the beach in silence, raised their arms, and exclaimed out, "God bless the King!"

Subsequently, they disappeared.

The survivors returned to the cape six weeks after they had initially escaped Wager Island. The sea was more untamed than it had ever been. Waves foamed like the jaws of a vast beast, while currents snarled and spat. Nevertheless, they were propelled by Cheap. They traversed the initial precipice. The subsequent step is the second. However, the oars in the men's palms became limp before they could clear the third. Weary. Defeated.

They silently sailed toward the surf. The breakers rose up like the fangs of judgment. "I believed that their objective was to immediately terminate their suffering and lives," Byron recollected. The silence became intolerable. Captain Cheap finally broke it. "Exert yourself with force," he directed. They complied, rowing only enough to direct the barge away from the boulders. However, continue no further. "We were now resigned to our fate," Byron wrote. There would be no further endeavors.

They retreated. Not out of optimism, but rather out of resignation. And as they returned to the estuary where the marines had been left, they prayed, perhaps naively, that they would find them alive.

There was only silence.

Laid on the shore was a solitary musket. There are no footprints. There is no sanctuary. Absence of human remains. Not even bones. Everything had been swept away by the breeze. The men stood silently, each one struggling with the intangible burden of their actions. Marine Bay was the name that Byron gave to the graveyard, which was devoid of burials.

Cheap begged for one final shove around the cape. He was certain that salvation was still elusive. However, no one followed. His obsession, which was once a source of inspiration, had now become a burden. The soldiers returned to the location from which they had attempted to escape for months—Wager Island. Campbell wrote, "We had now abandoned all hope of ever returning to our country of origin." The island, which was previously a penitentiary, had evolved into a form of sanctuary.

The return was delayed by nearly two weeks. The boats were scarcely able to maintain their integrity. Their sustenance was exhausted. In an act of desperation, Byron consumed the foul sealskin from his feet. the mind was distorted by hunger. He overheard the males conversing about the drawing of lots. This time, the purpose was not to scavenge from the deceased, but rather to eliminate one of them. To offer a living individual as a sacrifice for flesh. The unspoken line, which was already strained, was perilously close to breaking.

Lord Byron would subsequently immortalize the imagined ritual in verse:

The lots were generated, labeled, blended, and distributed.

In silent horror, and their distribution Lulled even the savage appetite which demanded, Like the Promethean vulture, this pollution.

However, they ultimately were unable to accomplish it.

Instead, they made one final ascent of Mount Misery. The decaying body of the man who had been murdered months prior—Mitchell's victim—was discovered by them. They were convinced that the man had been haunting them ever since. His body had survived in a location where countless others had perished.

His burial was conducted in stillness.

Then, they returned to their outpost by the shore, which had been blown away by the weather. The mist caused the shelters to sag. For once, the ocean was tranquil.

A long distance away, in England, the Admiralty awaited.

The court-martial would occur, and with it, the ultimate judgment—not only for Cheap and Bulkeley, but for all those who had survived. For the suffering they had endured. Additionally, their actions.

------- * * * -------

Chapter 20
THE DAY OF OUR DELIVERANCE

The Speedwell, groaning under its own wreckage, drifted eastward into the Strait of Magellan. Bulkeley, the self-appointed commander and navigator, leaned over the gunwales, his gaze fixed on a horizon that refused to be merciful. The boat, which was soaked with fear and patched with desperation, was unable to sail in close proximity to the breeze. "He wrote, defeated but still functional, 'It is enough to deject any thinking man.'" "The Speedwell, a wounded creature limping homeward, swam so poignant upon the sea," he observed.

Bulkeley depended on the shifting stars above, the battered log of Sir John Narborough, and fragments of memory in the absence of a proper chart. He measured latitude with a trembling sextant at night, shivering and sleep-deprived. During the day, he used dead reckoning to trace longitude, comparing the cliffs and currents to Narborough's drawings. The unknown was transformed into a navigable metaphor by his journal entries, which merged observation with poetry—"a point of land which makes like an old castle."

Wild, haunting terrain was traversed by them. The snow-laced Andes, blue-glassed glaciers, and wooded hills all stand as sentinels of an unresolved punishment. Two indigenous men, crowned in white feathers, lie prone and silent on a cliff, gazing down at the castaways before disappearing from sight. The sea narrowed and underwent a transformation at Cape Froward, the southernmost point of the continent. In this location, the Atlantic Ocean inhaled and the Pacific Ocean exhaled, as the two vast oceans squeezed together.

Bulkeley realized they had reached the junction when the waters twisted northeast. They were entering the renowned First Narrow of the Strait.

It was a location that had suffocated even the most powerful empires. The Spanish attempted to establish a settlement in the vicinity in 1584, which they referred to as the "Port Famine." Three hundred individuals, including Franciscan friars, soldiers, and infants. Starvation claimed virtually all. Corpses were discovered frozen in the cabins by subsequent explorers, and the air was reeking of decay. "They perished in the manner of dogs," stated a witness.

On December 7, 1741, Bulkeley's sailors passed Port Famine, which was two months after Wager Island. Their supplies were nearly exhausted. Their minds, which were already diminished, retreated even further inward. Then, a moment of hope appeared: guanacos were perched on a hillside. Reddish coats and fluid motion characterize these slender, deer-like ancestors of llamas. "Astonishingly rapid observation..." Bulkeley wrote, "They are extremely timid," as if they were prey. However, the williwaws howled down from the mountains and pushed the Speedwell off course when the castaways attempted to approach. The creatures disappeared into the trees.

The Strait has begun to diminish, with a maximum width of two miles right now. A constricted larynx. The tides rose by forty feet. From the cliffs, counterwinds were felt. The Speedwell entered this stretch at night, navigating between concealed shoals and black banks. They emerged at dawn, still afloat, albeit with a disheveled appearance.

Bulkeley observed the Cape of Eleven Thousand Virgins, a recognizable promontory, in the distance on December 11. In grander ships and with grander aspirations, they had passed it with Anson's squadron nearly a year prior. Suddenly, they emerged from the eastern mouth of the Strait and entered the vast Atlantic. They had accomplished it. With palms cracked and stomachs hollowed, they had traversed the 350-mile passage in thirty-one days in their wreck of a boat, surpassing even Magellan's armada.

However, there was no solace in store for them.

Rio Grande, Brazil, is the closest port, located more than sixteen hundred miles to the north. The Spanish patrol a harsh, unfamiliar littoral that lies between them. Capture may result in imprisonment or worse. Nevertheless, they were without sustenance. There is no alternative. They veered to the north.

Bulkeley navigated the Speedwell into Port Desire, a bay that Narborough had previously described. This occurred on December 16. He described a rock formation on the shore as resembling a stone sentinel, "much like a tower." The small island was discovered after they probed further and observed no Spanish activity. And there, seals laid unmoved and abundant, like relics of a bygone era.

The men entered the frigid shallows, with the water reaching their necks. Shoulders were adorned with firearms. Some were unable to swim at all. Although they were driven by starvation, they were like wolves. On the island, they engaged in a shootout with the lounging cattle and slaughtered what they could. Over an open flame, seal meat was seared. The castaways devoured it with hunger, their bodies trembling with relief.

Then, the process of death commenced.

At first, it struck in silence. Retching, collapse, and dizziness. Thomas Harvey, the purser, consumed an excessive amount of food and succumbed to his illness within hours. An additional individual pursued.

Although they were unaware of the term, it was refeeding syndrome. Bodies that were starved, when confronted with abrupt sustenance, reacted against themselves.

It had occurred previously in prisons, during sieges, and in colonies. This occurred once more, on an island inhabited by seals.

This was survival with fangs. A scar was left by each victory. Grief was present in every morsel.

Nevertheless, they persevered, rowing toward Rio Grande.

They had successfully evaded the island, the strait, and the promontory; however, they had not managed to escape the reckoning.

That occurred at a later date, in London.

In the Admiralty, testimony was recorded behind closed doors, amidst powdered wigs and ledgers. Captain Cheap would recount his narrative. Bulkeley would inform his. And in the midst of accusations of mutiny, cowardice, abandonment, and murder, the truth would glimmer and then recede somewhere between them.

However, one fact would be irrefutable:

They had successfully navigated the strait.

They were only able to confront a trial from which they could never genuinely escape.

They were nearly at the conclusion, yet they continued to suffer from hunger.

The Speedwell's seal meat reserves had exhausted themselves after weeks of drifting north along the South American coast. The final greasy fragments were the subject of an open fight among the men. Afterward, nothing occurred. Bulkeley, despite his swollen fingers and trembling limbs, continued to scratch ink into his journal, stating what was already widely understood: "To go from hence without meat or drink is certain death."

They were compelled to attempt an additional landing. However, the sea, which was both unpredictable and violent, pelted the shore with surges that were too powerful to approach. Bulkeley observed helplessly as he anchored in a remote location. The castaways were too traumatized to attempt swimming and were too feeble to do so. He was incapable of swimming. Nevertheless, a small number of individuals succeeded. The carpenter Cummins, the boatswain King, and an additional individual plunged into the surf. Subsequently, eleven additional individuals were inspired by that moment of courage—or perhaps mere desperation. John Duck, the free Black seaman whose endurance had earned him modest reverence, and Midshipman Isaac Morris were among them.

The surf was lethal. A single marine initiated a flailing motion. Morris attempted to locate him, but he submerged mere yards from the shore.

The remaining individuals crawled onto the dunes. Bulkeley threw four empty casks into the sea, lashing them with firearms. They were transported to the shore by the waves. The men hunted while filling the containers with water. They discovered a horse with the AR brand. The Spanish could not be far away. They killed, butchered, and cooked it. Subsequently, Cummins, King, and four other individuals returned by swimming with water and flesh.

However, a tempest struck as the remaining members of the landing party prepared to return.

The Speedwell was compelled to depart from the shore, causing it to spiral out into the gray chop. Bulkeley returned the gaze. He could still see them—Duck, Morris, and six others—stranded, waving from the beach, out of reach. "We continue to observe the individuals on the shore, but we are unable to remove them," he stated.

The rudder fractured that evening. Steering became nearly impossible.

Bulkeley assembled Baynes, Cummins, and the other individuals on board. On the coast of South America, they formulated an additional desperate agreement on January 14, 1742. It was stated that they were concerned that the vessel would capsize at any moment and that continuing to remain would result in "perishment." They enclosed their justification in a barrel containing ammunition and a letter, and threw it into the ocean.

The marooned men fell to their knees upon discovering the container and reading it.

The situation deteriorated on the Speedwell, which was drifting. The food had vanished. Water is almost there. Bulkeley stated that only fifteen of the men were still capable of moving, if "people may be called healthy that are scarce able to crawl." Even he, who was once the strongest, was unable to stand properly. Less was said by them. Complained more.

Baynes, who was ailing and in decline, composed a narrative about the men who were dying in his vicinity, their hollow eyes passively pleading for assistance. On January 23, Thomas Clark, who had safeguarded his son for months, passed away. The following day, his son followed suit. Thomas Maclean, an eighty-two-year-old servant who had endured shipwrecks, scurvy, and tempests, passed away on the 25th.

Now scarcely coherent, Bulkeley continued to force words onto the page. At one time, he was under the impression that he had observed butterflies falling from the heavens.

Afterward, there is salvation.

The Speedwell was directed toward a broad river outlet on January 28. Through crusted eyelashes, Bulkeley gazed. Initially, he believed it to be a hallucination. Subsequently, rooftops were evident. Homes constructed from wood. Human existence.

Rio Grande, Brazil, was the location.

He raised his voice. Individuals who were still alive were roused. They guided the wreck to port by grasping the sails that were left.

The docks were filled with the murmur of disbelief as the townspeople congregated. They observed as a vessel that was plagued, with its sails shredded and its hull rotting, drifted into view. The following scene caused them to shrink back.

The men—if they could be classified as such—were stacked on top of one another like cargo, their skin scorched and peeling, and their features were skeletal. Hair that has been coated with salt. Sunken and inflamed eyes.

Bulkeley was the sole survivor.

He informed them that they were the final survivors of HMS Wager.

Crossing himself was the governor's action. He murmured, "A miracle."

The ailing were transported to a hospital by physicians. William Oram, the carpenter's companion who had assisted in the construction of the Speedwell, passed away shortly thereafter.

Eighty-one sailors had departed from Wager Island. All that was left was twenty-nine.

Even one survivor was evidence of God to Bulkeley. He designated January 28 as the day of our liberation. He wrote with fervor, "It should be recollected in this manner." He was of the opinion that only an imbecile could deny divine providence in light of the ordeal they had experienced.

Clean mattresses were provided to the survivors. Bread plates. Beef. Wine. Bulkeley acknowledged in his journal, "We believe ourselves to be quite content."

Bulkeley wrote that the inhabitants of Brazil traveled to witness them, as pilgrims to the wreck and this marvel. The Speedwell was transported to land, where it was preserved as a symbol of perseverance and hardship.

However, the conflict—known as the War of Jenkins' Ear—persisted. Bulkeley communicated with a British officer stationed in Rio de Janeiro. In the letter, he included a concluding, cryptic note:

"Captain Cheap has remained behind at his own request."

For what reason?

The query would reverberate throughout the Atlantic, reaching the courtrooms of London.

For the reason that there would be a trial. A moment of truth. A confrontation that is not solely between survivors, but also between competing truths: justice and remorse, loyalty and mutiny, survival and betrayal.

The final, shocking truths of the Wager's voyage would be revealed before the British Admiralty tribunal.

------- * * * -------

Part Five
Judgment

Chapter 21
A LITERARY REBELLION

For the first time in months, John Bulkeley permitted himself to take a walk without dread in the tranquil warmth of a Brazilian evening. He strolled through the countryside near their new lodging, a modest home that had been lent to them by benevolent locals, with a companion by his side and the freedom of the open road beneath his feet. However, the instant they returned, that tranquility was shattered. The mechanisms had been compromised.

His room was a state of disarray, with drawers being yanked and papers being dispersed. A search had been conducted by an individual. Then, a commotion was heard. Two individuals surged forward. Someone struck Bulkeley in the mandible. He responded by retaliating. The attackers fled into the night after a tumultuous conflict.

However, Bulkeley had observed one of their visages. A fellow castaway. A man who was renowned for fulfilling the orders of the boatswain, John King, who had previously struck Captain Cheap in the face during the infamous mutiny on Wager Island. This was not a robbery. This was a cautionary tale.

They were not seeking sustenance or valuables. It was Bulkeley's journal.

The sole contemporaneous account of the catastrophe, the mutiny, and the events that transpired.

Bulkeley and his most devoted associates relocated to a remote fishing village amid feelings of unease. "We believed ourselves to be secure and protected in this location," he wrote.

They were not.

A few evenings later, the door was pounded by fists. Entry was demanded by a group of males. Bulkeley declined. He responded with a subdued, yet resolute, voice, "It is an inappropriate time of the night." The volume of the pounding increased. The castaways, in a state of panic, searched the home for weapons. They managed to flee by scaling a wall in the rear, as they were unable to locate any.

It was evident that the journal was no longer merely a diary. It was both a weapon and a target. Bulkeley had documented identities, actions, and decisions. It could all unravel if Cheap were ever discovered, or if another survivor provided a different account. King had vowed to retrieve the journal "or take our lives," and whispers began to circulate.

Even the Brazilian officials were taken aback. One individual observed, "How peculiar it is that individuals who had endured numerous adversities and hardships were unable to reach a mutually beneficial agreement." However, the existing divisions had been further exacerbated by the hardship. The events that transpired on Wager Island had followed them to the shore.

Lieutenant Baynes, the most senior officer among them, had become increasingly distrustful and reclusive. Bulkeley was informed of rumors that Baynes was clandestinely informing the authorities that Bulkeley and Cummins had orchestrated the mutiny, ensnared Cheap, and abandoned him.

As a result, Bulkeley proceeded with his customary practice of writing.

Bulkeley accused Baynes of "false and vile allegations" in a formal letter and reminded him that in England, they would all be required to "give account of [their] actions, and justice take place."

Baynes did not delay.

In March 1742, he discretely departed Brazil aboard a vessel that was en route to England. His goal was to arrive first in order to present his perspective on the narrative to the Admiralty.

Bulkeley and Cummins required several months to obtain their own passage. British merchants in Portugal warned them along the way that Baynes had already made incriminating claims against them. Some even advised the duo to avoid returning to England, fearing that they would be executed for mutiny.

But Bulkeley presented his journal to the merchants—the very object King had attempted to steal—and informed them that "the individual who accused us was the ringleader if there was any mutiny." He reminded them that Baynes had not maintained a journal. In an effort to keep his life, Bulkeley had taken a risk.

He and Cummins continued to advance. Bulkeley wrote, "We were adamant about our innocence and resolute in our commitment to represent our nation at all events."

Their vessel arrived at Portsmouth on January 1, 1743.

England was imminent. Similarly, their residences were. Bulkeley had not seen his wife or five children in more than two years.

However, they were halted by the Navy.

Onboard, they were apprehended.

Baynes had already conveyed a notarized statement to the Admiralty. In it, he asserted that Bulkeley and Cummins had commanded a group of mutineers that captured and incapacitated Captain Cheap, subsequently abandoning him on Wager Island. The Admiralty ordered Bulkeley and Cummins to be held under guard exclusively on the basis of that allegation. The two men had endured storms, malnutrition, and a three-thousand-mile sea voyage, only to be imprisoned in their own country.

Bulkeley did not simply submit a letter when requested to provide his account of the events.

He provided them with everything.

The complete journal. The unfiltered, daily account of their voyage. He included Cummins as a coauthor as a sign of loyalty and strategy, as two voices were more difficult to dismiss than one. Bulkeley detailed Captain Cheap's disintegration in the journal. The murder of Cozens. The descent into disorder. "We were compelled to abandon the common road by necessity," he wrote. "Our case was unique... Our primary concern was the preservation of our lives and liberties."

Bulkeley submitted the signed documents generated on the island, one of which bore Baynes's signature, in addition to the journal. In legalistic language, these documents, which were composed during periods of crisis, provided a detailed account of their decisions and justifications.

The journal was returned by the Admiralty due to its overwhelming size. They instructed Bulkeley to compose a summary that would be "a narrative abstract that would not be overly tedious for their Lordships to review."

He yielded.

He stated in the cover note that they had "strictly adhered to the intention of the unfortunate Captain Cheap, whose final directive was to provide a dependable account to your Lordships."

The journal was perused by the Lords of the Admiralty. They reviewed Baynes's declaration. And they were unable to progress.

There was no information regarding Cheap.

They would not render judgment until he could be declared deceased or return to speak for himself. The inquiry was postponed.

Cummins and Bulkeley were released after a two-week period.

When they returned home, their families were taken aback. Bulkeley wrote, "Our families had long abandoned us as lost." "They perceived us as sons, husbands, and fathers who had been miraculously restored to them."

However, the marvel was not accompanied by a verdict.

A court-martial would not be conducted. There is no formal exoneration. No public remorse.

Silence.

In that silence, the truth of Wager Island was shattered—between memories and journals, between the living and the deceased, between loyalty and survival.

The wreckage persisted, despite the conclusion of the accident.

John Bulkeley had endured a three-thousand-mile voyage in a boat that was flooding, as well as a shipwreck and mutiny. However, upon his return to England, he was struck by a more tranquil and unforgiving storm: bureaucratic purgatory. Despite his survival, there were no celebrations, accolades, or feelings of relief. His compensation was concealed by the Admiralty. He was prohibited from participating in additional naval operations. His life was suspended, as if guilt could be inferred from indecision, despite the fact that no official judgment had been rendered on his alleged crimes.

Bulkeley wrote regretfully, "A remnant of us are returned to our native country after surviving the loss of the ship and combating with famine and innumerable difficulties." However, we remain unfortunate, unemployed, and nearly without assistance, even in this location.

He was a sailor without a ship, a gunner without a cannon. He requested permission from the Admiralty to assume the role of captaining a merchant vessel from Plymouth to London. "In order to prevent your Lordships from imagining that I had fled from justice," he wrote. "I am willing and eager to comply with the most stringent evaluation of my conduct in relation to Captain Cheap." He was unable to protect himself from destitution, despite his obligation to do so. Authorization was granted. Money was not present.

Bulkeley would employ language to combat what he was unable to combat with rank.

Consequently, he initiated a new rebellion, this time without the use of muskets or mutiny, but rather with ink. He initiated the process of preparing his journal for publication. He would take his case to the court of public opinion if the Admiralty failed to restore his name.

No one had ever heard of it. Accounts of their exploits were occasionally published by naval officers. However, how is it possible for a gunner and a carpenter to publish a comprehensive sea narrative? Incredibly scandalous. Bulkeley composed an audacious preface in anticipation of the backlash:

He acknowledged that "we do not establish institutions for naturalists and men of great learning," but "individuals who possess a shared understanding are capable of recording daily observations, particularly those that they have personally contributed significantly to."

He anticipated allegations of betrayal. "It has been suggested to us that the publication of this journal would offend certain individuals of distinction," he wrote. However, the Wager was already well-known to humanity. "Is it considered an offense to disclose that we were shipwrecked and returned home in a state of poverty akin to that of beggars?"

His demeanor was populist and defiant. "Are we to be intimidated by the possibility of offending the—Lord knows whom?", as we have encountered mortality in a variety of forms?

He defended the leadership of himself and Cummins on the island. "The reader will discover that our necessity was absolutely compelling, despite the fact that our confining the Captain is considered an audacious and unprecedented action." Bulkeley described the narrative as "a plain maritime style," a modern voice that was unsentimental, unpolished, and alive with the grit of the lower decks. It was not embellished with miracle tales or exotic marvel.

The public's appetite for the narrative of HMS Wager was insatiable by the time they were prepared to sell it. They sold the manuscript to a London bookseller for an amount they described as "considerable." However, it was an uncommon triumph for two beggars of fortune—although it would not rescue them from financial ruin.

The book, A Voyage to the South-Seas, in the Years 1740–1, was released six months after Bulkeley and Cummins returned to the stalls.

Everything was promised on the title page:

"An accurate account of the Wager, His Majesty's ship, their valiant quest for freedom, their passage through the Straits of Magellan, and the extraordinary hardships they encountered due to a lack of food."

It was sold for three shillings and sixpence per copy. The journal was an immediate phenomenon after it was serialized in The London Magazine.

However, not all were satisfied.

The Admiralty and the aristocracy were enraged. In Bulkeley, a Lord Commissioner was photographed:

"How dare you publicly impugn a gentleman's character?"

A naval officer vented his frustrations to the Universal Spectator:

"If Captain Cheap returns home, he will remove the censure and reimpose it on the disobedience of his subordinates."

Once more, there were murmurs of execution. Bulkeley had now engaged in sedition through the printing press, in addition to mutiny.

Nevertheless, the book persevered.

Subsequently, a historian commended it for encapsulating "a genuine searing in every page." The public opinion was influenced by the unvarnished, unapologetic tone. Even some of the "gold-braided gentry" reluctantly acknowledged that its "gallant pugnacity" was irrefutable.

Captain Cheap had yet to make an appearance.

Additionally, there was no official counternarrative.

Bulkeley's narrative was adopted as the narrative in the absence of a competing narrative. He had not only survived the voyage, but he had also penned the initial draft of history.

He and Cummins were prohibited from serving as naval commanders. They continued to be impoverished.

However, they were unrestricted.

Additionally, the journal that nearly resulted in their deaths had become their savior.

Nevertheless, Bulkeley was aware that reprieves were never permanent. Just as he had on the island, in Brazil, and on the Speedwell, he sensed the next tempest brewing.

Because there were now murmurs circulating in the pressrooms and coffeehouses of London, rumors that Commodore George Anson, the individual who had initiated the ill-fated expedition, was alive. That his vessel had traversed the Pacific. That he was returning home with both truth and treasure.

Perhaps the apparition of Captain Cheap will accompany him.

------- * * * -------

Chapter 22
THE PRIZE

Anson's silhouette was etched against a vast canvas of restless sea off the southeastern coast of China as he stood erect upon the quarterdeck of the Centurion. April of 1743 marked the two-year anniversary of the Wager's disappearance, and not a single murmur had been heard since. There is no devastation. There are no survivors. Only silence. The Pearl and the Severn, those once-promising companions of war, had limped home after fleeing Cape Horn's merciless wrath. They perceived their retreat as disgrace rather than strategy, as their captains were consumed by humiliation and scurvy. Nevertheless, Anson, who had been tempered by adversity and seasoned by suffering, had never spoken negatively of them. He had also experienced the Horn's blind animosity and was aware of its ability to demolish even the most resolute of individuals.

The shattered remnants of his once-proud squadron had endeavored to unite in the mystical embrace of the Juan Fernández Islands. However, they were gradually erased by the passage of time, disease, and the sea. The Anna, a modest cargo vessel, had been cannibalized and abandoned on the ocean. The Trial, rendered ineffective in combat and haunted by death, was abandoned to decay. And the Gloucester, a noble and revered vessel, had exhaled her last breath when she was unable to further restrain the ocean. Her crew, who were half-dead and scarcely able to walk, were lifted onto the Centurion like corpses, their bones protruding through the loose skin and their breath thick with decay.

As Anson issued the directive to destroy the Gloucester, her weapons discharged fire. Lawrence Millechamp, the purser, described the ship as "a grand, horrid appearance," with her loaded cannons discharging in solemn intervals—"like mourning guns." Lieutenant Philip Saumarez described the scene as "as melancholy a scene as I ever observed." The concluding explosion occurred at dawn. The powder room erupted, accompanied by a final salute to a vessel that was once praised as the jewel of the English navy.

However, Anson refused to withdraw. He had lost ships, men, time, and nearly hope, but he had not lost his purpose. He continued his journey across the Pacific, accompanied by only the Centurion and 227 emaciated soldiers, the majority of whom were young boys. They captured a few Spanish merchantmen and sacked a lonely Peruvian outpost, victories that were so meager that they felt like consolation prizes distributed before the conclusion of a play. Then, scurvy returned, more vicious than ever before. Its symptoms were now recognized, and its repercussions were no less dreadful. Clusters of males perished. Each day, six, eight, or twelve bodies were discarded overboard. One sailor reported that they reeked of "rotten sheep." The surviving and the dying, both shrunken and gray, slept next to each other.

Anson carried the weight of failure in his bosom like ballast. "If I believed that I had devalued the public's regard, I would experience immense distress upon my return to my homeland," he wrote. He was scarcely able to man the sails, let alone mount a fight, as two thousand had been reduced to two hundred.

His troops, however, continued to remain. Yes, they complained; however, they submitted. He ruled with resolve, rather than a lash. He did not coerce them into loyalty; rather, he encouraged it. An officer subsequently stated that Anson's composure during the catastrophe was so unyielding that "we could not for shame betray any great dejection."

Then, the tempest occurred.

One day after anchoring near an uninhabited Pacific island, the Centurion disappeared from sight. Anson observed his final hope vanish beyond the horizon while ashore with a detached attitude. They were stranded for days, a fate that mirrored that of the Wager. Despair grasped at their throats. The group's transformation was characterized by Millechamp as follows: "Grief, discontent, terror, and despair were evident in the expressions of each of us."

Anson refused to await death and instead directed the transformation of a small transport craft into a temporary vessel. He told them, "We must dedicate ourselves to the task at hand, unless we wish to conclude our lives in this untamed environment." And so they did. The commodore, unwavering, worked alongside the most vulnerable sailor, hoisting, hammering, and persevering. Their salvation was the result of their unity, which was borne out of desperation.

And then, as if summoned by a sailor's supplication, the Centurion reappeared.

The reunion was miraculous, emotional, and jubilant. The Centurion, who was alive but had sustained injuries, had fought to return to her master. The journey was resumed.

As they cut through the South China Sea, Anson assembled his crew, which had been battered. He gazed at the faces that had aged decades in months, their sunburnt skin and hollow cheekbones betraying their youth, as he stood atop his cabin. Anson had sown a seed: a lie—but more significantly, they had restocked and repaired in Canton.

He had communicated that they were returning home, their mission completed, and their spirits weary. The Spanish governor of Manila had already expressed his satisfaction in dispatches: "The English are weary of their endeavor, having achieved nothing."

Anson's voice echoed, "Gentlemen..." I have summoned you to inform you of our obligations. He hesitated.

"Do not travel to England!"

Stirring ensued among the males. Eyes expanded. Was this act of insanity or a demonstration of resolve?

The commodore disclosed his final card. It was not a surrender; it was a strategic decision. He had ascertained the probable path of the fabled Manila galleon, a floating cathedral of silk and bullion. He was of the opinion that it would soon be visible off the coast of the Philippines, based on timing, rumors in Chinese ports, and patterns. And it was his intention to intercept it.

Their prey was formidable—galleons were reputed to be invincible, their hulls were as hard as iron, and their treasure was unimaginable. However, Anson's irises were ablaze with an intensity that no cannon could quench. "That spirit within you, my friends," he exclaimed, "is sufficient to secure victory."

It was the ultimate wager of a gambler. However, Anson was not a naive individual. His mission, which was previously consumed by sorrow and dispersed across oceans, now had a single, unwavering objective: redemption.

The men erupted in cheers, waving hats, fists, and aspirations to the sky. If this were to be their final journey, they would not encounter it as castaways or corpses, but as warriors, who were contending not only for plunder but also for purpose.

Consequently, the Centurion continued to sail, not toward his homeland, but toward legend.

The wind carried them toward Samar Island, a remote, volcanic island rimmed in coral, as Anson stood at the helm of the Centurion, its bow cutting east through aquamarine waters. Anson had reason to believe that fate, his long-standing adversary, might eventually encounter him on the island, which was the third-largest in the Philippines.

The tropical sun had scorched his troops, and they were hollowed out by fever and scurvy. Nevertheless, Anson did not allow them to rest. He instructed them to "prepare or perish," and they complied. The brutal rhythm of each day was consistent: muskets sounded like thunder as they struck decapitated targets that were suspended from the yardarms. The deck was shook by the recoil of the cannons as they boomed in coordinated passes. In mock boarding exercises, sailors wielded swords and cutlasses. Upon completion, they repeated the entire process. More rapidly. More precise. Anson reminded them that a single error would result in their being thrown into the sea, either shattered or incinerated.

Cape Espiritu Santo was observed by an observer on May 20. The northern boundary of Samar was delineated by the jagged promontory, which protruded into the sea in the shape of a blade. Anson promptly ordered the topgallant sails to be furled in order to reduce their profile. They would remain in suspense. A ship that appears to be in shadow on the horizon. The Spanish were unable to anticipate their arrival.

They patrolled the waters like spirits for weeks. They alternated between surveying the seas by day and sweating under the tropical glare as they moved back and forth. At night, the constellations appeared to be somewhat blurry due to fatigue. Lieutenant Saumarez recorded in his journal, "Exercising our men at their quarters, with great anticipation..." Maintaining our positions and maintaining an external gaze. However, anticipation began to transform into uncertainty. The enemy had not yet arrived. The sea did not indicate that it would ever do so.

The crew was on the brink of collapse by June 20. This was not due to a lack of courage, but rather to an excessive amount of waiting. The exercises no longer elicited adrenaline; rather, they caused a dull ache in the arms and backs of men who had long since abandoned their hopes. The faces became pale. Sunken eyes developed. Saumarez grimly observed, "All hands began to appear very melancholy."

However, at 5:40 a.m. that morning, an event occurred that disrupted the incantation.

A sharp, electric exclamation from the mast: "Sails ho!" A single particle. Then, additional information. White topgallants are visible on the southeast horizon, emitting a faint radiance in the new sun. Anson made a sudden move toward his telescope. Large and with broad beams, the vessel was substantial. He had not yet acquired a flag; however, it was unnecessary. He was aware. This was her.

The Manila galleon.

Isolated.

Upon receiving the command "Clear for action!" the Centurion was propelled into action. Millechamp stated, "Our vessel immediately developed into a ferment." "Every man was prepared to lend a hand, and everyone believed that the task could not be successfully completed without his involvement." The deck appeared to have been impacted by lightning.

In order to accommodate the weapons, the walls of the cabins were demolished. The livestock was thrown overboard, including honking waterfowl and squealing goats. Spare timber, tools, and crates—anything that could potentially serve as shrapnel—were thrown into the sea. The deck was sanded to prevent blood from smearing it in the future.

The gun crews below were busy preparing their stations, which included rammers, sponges, wads, horns, and iron bars—creating an orchestra of devastation. Buckets of seawater were arranged in anticipation of a conflagration. Powder monkeys, boys who were no older than fifteen, received gunpowder cartridges and sprinted barefoot up ladders, diving beneath the beams to avoid falling. Just one spark could transform them into debris.

George Allen prepared his primitive surgery in the ship's belly, past the nauseating aroma of tar and perspiration. Allen, who was previously a surgeon's mate, is now the superintendent by attrition. He arranged linen bandages, knives, and saws. A temporary operating table was constructed by dragging sea containers. A sail canvas was extended across the floor to collect the blood, as it was anticipated that there would be a substantial amount of it.

The men proceeded with a somber determination. They were not merely contending for their country or for money. They were advocating for the right to return—alive and with something to demonstrate the extent of the suffering they had endured. The galleon symbolized more than just Spanish riches. Revenge was the motivation. Salvation. In the culminating act of a tragedy that had spanned oceans.

The men knew the moment had arrived as the Centurion surged toward her objective, guns prepared, sails straining, and hearts pounding.

They had traveled halfway around the globe. They had observed their companions perish in every conceivable manner, including starvation, scurvy, storm, and despair. They would either conclude the event in triumph or perish in flames.

Anson remained unreadable, vigilant, and composed in the midst of it all. His eyes, which were perpetually on the alert, alternated between the sky and the sea, the wind and the sails, and destiny and fire. He had anticipated this moment for two years. He was now confronted with the situation.

The galleon was struck by the entire weight of the Centurion as it passed behind him, as if in judgment.

Nuestra Señora de Covadonga—Our Lady of Covadonga—was the name of the Spanish galleon, which was both revered and cursed by the sailors who served aboard it. Under the command of the seasoned Captain Gerónimo Montero, the ship had transformed into a floating citadel of

Spanish pride, shrouded in its divine namesake and loaded with treasure. Montero had navigated her decks for fourteen years. He was prepared to sacrifice her in a blaze of fire and blood, as he was now ordered to either defend her to the death or annihilate her before surrender.

Upon the Centurion's pursuit, the galleon's crew recognized the imminent peril. Nevertheless, Montero refrained from participating in the race. It is possible that he misjudged the Centurion's condition, assuming that she was too beaten up to engage in combat. Perhaps it was a matter of honor. Whatever the case, he directed his vessel directly into the course of the British warship—an action that could be interpreted as either brave or fatalistic.

Anson maintained his position on the quarterdeck, his telescope affixed to the galleon's approaching silhouette. He observed that its size was smaller than that of the Centurion, and its armament was as follows: thirty-two cannons to his sixty, with the largest being no more than twelve pounds, in contrast to his twenty-four. The Centurion ought to have crushed her on paper.

However, Anson encountered an issue that could not be resolved through numerical calculations: personnel. The Covadonga accommodated 530 individuals, which was more than 300 more than Anson's inadequate personnel. His own soldiers were emaciated, ill, and fatigued from combat. It was impossible to load and discharge each cannon due to a lack of personnel. Consequently, Anson adjusted.

He assigned only two men to each starboard cannon, one to load and the other to scrub, rather than full gun crews. Several twelve-man squads would sprint between the guns, discharge them in sequence, and then continue their journey, leaving the loaders to prepare the next round. It was a risky endeavor—a ballet of violence that was propelled by desperation.

Another tactical maneuver was executed by him. Anson had observed the galleon's low gunwales, which left its officers at risk of exposure. He positioned his most talented sharpshooters in the mast tops, armed with muskets and prepared to shower death from the sky.

Montero, on the other hand, emulated his adversary. He emptied his decks by hurling livestock into the sea and positioned armed men in the rigging. He raised the crimson Spanish regal flag, which was embroidered with castles and lions, as the distance decreased. Anson responded by hoisting the British flag, and both commanders opened their gunports.

A single discharge. Then another. It was not yet lethal, but the echoes across the sea were sufficient to convey a message. The genuine conflict was imminent.

Nature turned against the ships as they approached within three miles of one another just past noon. The sea was pelted with rain as a tempest erupted from the heavens. Mist enveloped the atmosphere, resulting in a loss of visibility. The Covadonga, invisible but advancing, was concealed within the deluge. She approached the British each time they caught a glimpse.

Two kilometers. One. One half mile.

Ice-eyed, Anson directed his troops to cease their fire. Not yet. Not until they could smell the enemy's breath.

The rain ceased. The sea subsided into a gleaming menace. Finally, the Covadonga was visible from a distance of less than one hundred yards. Her cannons were exposed. Her sails are fully extended. Her decks are roiled with bodies. Anson meticulously adjusted the Centurion's sails to prevent the hull from being exposed to a fatal strike, as the breeze died. He then executed a daring maneuver by crossing the Covadonga's wake and swinging alongside her, windward and in control.

Fifty meters.

Twenty-five.

His soldiers were frozen, their breath was shallow, and their hands were gripping ropes and fuses. The signal was then issued by Anson.

Explosion.

The masts were the first to erupt. Sharpshooters fired, their muskets cracking and smoke billowing in their faces as they targeted Montero's men in the rigging. The air was transformed into a maelstrom of splinters and iron. Muskets were discharged, reloaded, and fired again with brutal efficiency. The sails were shredded above. The ropes broke like whips. Lead tore flesh and bone, causing men to shriek.

The cannons erupted at sea level.

The broadside of Montero made a thunderous sound, launching a complete wall of destruction simultaneously. In contrast, Anson's unconventional approach generated a continuous stream of fire. A cannon was discharged by one unit, which then closed the port. The squad sprinted to the next station while the loaders swabbed the steaming container. discharge, reload, discharge again—a rhythm summoned from the underworld.

Millechamp wrote, "The cannon's thunder was so rapid that it produced a continuous sound." Both ships were enveloped in smoke. The air was choked with powder and cries.

Anson, armed with a sword, maintained a vigil on the quarterdeck. He observed a faint glimmer of fire through the haze of conflict. The

Covadonga's stern had been set on fire. Her mizzenmast was consumed by flames, which caused widespread anxiety. However, the galleon's sailors resisted, removing the burning rigging and discarding it into the sea.

In the interim, mortality descended without regard for individuality.

A chain projectile from the Covadonga tore through the rigging of the Centurion. Her hull was punctured by lead projectiles. Following the impact of cannonballs below the waterline, the carpenter's crew promptly repaired any breaches before the sea could claim them. Thomas Richmond, a sailor, was immediately decapitated. An additional individual sustained an injury to their limb. As he was hurried beneath the deck, blood spurted from the limb.

In the ship's bowels, surgeon George Allen was encircled by chaos as he stood over an operating table constructed from sea chests. Without anesthesia, he steadied his hands and sawed through flesh and bone as cannon fire rocked the hull. The lesion was cauterized by the application of boiling tar. Nevertheless, the individual passed away.

Allen was surrounded by wounded sailors who wailed and grasped his arms, pleading for relief as he labored on another. He later recollected, "Some of them poured forth the most piercing cries, while others grabbed my arms... even as I was passing the needle."

The floors were black with powder as seen above. The men fought as if they were possessed, their shirts soaked in blood and perspiration. The Centurion's teeth and bones were rattled by the recoil of her weapons, which caused her to rock. Splinters dispersed in a manner reminiscent of daggers. Red was the color of the decks.

Nevertheless, they continued to engage in conflict.

Anson was aware that this was not merely a conflict over treasure. It was the culmination of a journey that was characterized by death, sorrow, and shame. A reckoning was in order.

The Centurion would either emerge victorious or join her ghosted sisters in the depths.

Anson witnessed the moment he had awaited for years: a solitary, bloodied figure staggering toward the tattered Spanish royal flag, scarcely fading after the final cannon blast. The galleon Covadonga, which was once a floating citadel, was currently lying still and shattered. her sails were shredded to ribbons, her masts were cracked, and her hull was gaping with wounds. The man reached the mainmast and proceeded to lower the flag before either side could fire again. The red-and-gold standard of Spain gradually descended, as silence settled over the devastation like fog. The Centurion's troops were astonished and incredulous, standing motionless. It had concluded.

Captain Gerónimo Montero, who was oblivious of the surrender, had issued a final command of defiance below deck: detonate the powder room and descend with dignity. He instructed an adjacent officer to sink the vessel. However, the stranger hesitated, his eyes fixed on the smoke-stained ceiling. "It is too late," he replied.

Lieutenant Saumarez was dispatched to seize control of the Covadonga. Even the hardened mariners of the Centurion were shaken by the discovery he made. There were entrails and torn limbs strewn throughout the decks, which were slippery with blood. There was an unpleasant odor of decay and powder in the air. A British sailor subsequently admitted that the sight of such sights made victory seem hollow to any individual of a "humane disposition." Three lives had been lost by Anson's crew. The Spanish had sustained over eighty wounds and lost nearly seventy soldiers.

However, Anson did not exhibit any triumphant cruelty. He despatched his own surgeon to provide medical attention to the Spanish wounded, which included Montero, who was alive despite his injuries. The prisoners were handled with respect. Saumarez reassured them, "You fought with courage." "You will receive a satisfactory manner of treatment."

Then, the instant that would alter the course of history occurred.

Saumarez and his men cautiously navigated the splintered beams, shattered chests, and water pooling from the breached hull of the galleon, using lanterns to descend into the ruined hold. Initially, the scene was characterized by disorder, with crates of cheese, sacks of grain, and tumbling crates. However, as one individual reached into a sack, his hand encountered a cold, metallic object that was concealed beneath the oil. Preserve.

Subsequently, they discovered additional information. Cracked but intact, a vessel was filled with gold dust. Bags were overflowing with silver coinage, numbering in the hundreds of thousands. Bells, bowls, and rough slabs of virgin silver were discovered in concealed compartments. False-bottomed trunks were opened to disclose riches beyond imagination, and jewels were discovered concealed beneath floorboards. In total, it was the most substantial maritime treasure ever captured by a British naval commander, with a current value exceeding $80 million.

Anson had done what no other Englishman of his generation had accomplished: he had circumnavigated the globe in conflict, defeated a superior force, and captured the gold of an empire.

The Centurion returned home on June 15, 1744, one year after sailing up the Channel.

The War of Jenkins' Ear had yielded scant positive news for Britain. The majority of offensives had resulted in defeat, disease, and devastation. However, Anson's victory was as sudden as a thunderclap. The London press proclaimed "GREAT BRITAIN'S TRIUMPH."

The streets were brimming with citizens who were ecstatic. Anson and his remaining men led thirty-two wagons that were each under armed security and were loaded with treasure in a grand procession. A prize of nearly £300 was awarded to a marine, which was sufficient to fund his retirement. Anson was promoted to rear admiral, awarded over £90,000, and welcomed into the royal court as a hero.

The parade proceeded across Fulham Bridge, passing through Piccadilly, St. James's, and Pall Mall, with the accompaniment of French horns and trumpets. Anson stood beside the Prince and Princess of Wales at the center of the celebration, his face expressionless and his eyes adrift as he observed the throng that erupted in appreciation of his name. The scene was compared to ancient Rome by one observer, who noted that the spoils of war were trailed behind the victors as they returned from conquest. In fact, this triumph—which was so cinematic in its scope—was not solely military in nature. It was emblematic. It restored the prestige of a nation.

The taverns and alleys of London were soon filled with the reverberations of a well-known sea ballad:

"The wagon loads of money arrive, / And they are all seized by the brave Anson."

The entire nation sang. It appeared that the conflict had a hero.

Nevertheless, not all individuals who had sailed with the squadron were able to reclaim their former renown.

In March 1746, two years later, a battered vessel entered the harbor at Dover. A man who appeared gaunt and austere approached the shore, his eyes piercing and his mouth razor-sharp. It was Captain David Cheap, the long-lost commander of the Wager, the ship that had splintered on the rocks of South America and was destined to vanish into myth.

He was followed by two survivors: Lieutenant Thomas Hamilton and Midshipman John Byron. They were the final shards of a disbanded crew—the honor guard of a phantom ship.

And they brought with them a tale that was more sinister than gold: a tale of betrayal, starvation, mutiny, and murder, as well as a secret that would plunge the empire into scandal.

Glory had been conveyed by the galleon.

However, the Wager was on the brink of rendering a decision.

------- * * * -------

Chapter 23
Grub Street Hacks

Five and a half years. That was the duration of their absence. The gaunt and ghostlike Captain David Cheap, Lieutenant Thomas Hamilton, and Midshipman John Byron, who were presumed dead and buried in the nation's memory, now walked ashore at Dover, their eyes reflecting oceans of anguish. They had been lamented by England. It now stood in a state of awe, as if the sea had vomited out three Lazaruses to recount a story that no one had anticipated.

They arrived with a survival narrative that was so peculiar and brutal that it would render the splendor of Anson's treasure fleet seem false in comparison. The three survivors began to recount the events that had transpired in courtrooms and naval offices, in front of officials and correspondents. Their focus was not only on the lost ship Wager, but also on the moral compass of each man who had been left stranded on that forsaken shore.

Two dugout canoes and a company of native Patagonians arrived days after their unsuccessful attempt to escape Wager Island, following the burial of a murdered companion. This provided a brief moment of hope. Martin, a Chono seafarer who spoke Spanish, was one of them. He offered them a shot at salvation. He would direct them north to Chiloé Island, the nearest Spanish outpost, in exchange for their final remaining vessel, the barge. They consented due to their limited options.

They embarked on March 6, 1742. However, optimism was as fragile as ever. While the majority of the castaways explored the shore for food, six of them betrayed them by stealing the barge and disappearing into the wilderness. Cheap referred to it as "cowardice." However, Midshipman Campbell had overheard their murmurs. They did not express dread; rather, they sought to escape from their "monomaniacal" captain. The truth was painful.

The castaways, who were now reduced to ten individuals, embarked on a perilous voyage northward by climbing into the canoes of the Chono. Their extremities trembled, and their stomachs were hollow. Death claimed them one by one. Before Byron's eyes, surgeon Elliot, who was once a pillar of fortitude, withered. He collapsed on a barren stretch of coastline. He presented Campbell with his pocket watch, which was his sole item of value, as his final act. They excavated his grave in solitude and sand.

The voyage transitioned from the sea to the swamp when only five individuals remained: Cheap, Byron, Campbell, Hamilton, and Martin. The Chono guided them along a concealed path that traversed eight miles of soggy wilderness. They disassembled their canoes and transported the components on their backs. Except for Cheap, all bear weight. He had begun to unravel, stockpiling food scraps and muttering nonsense. He shuffled like a phantom between life and death, physically devastated and mentally unraveling.

Byron, too, experienced difficulties. He contemplated surrendering, simply dissolving into a state of abyss as he collapsed beneath a tree. However, there was a ragtag thread of will within him that remained steadfast. "These reflections would not provide any resolution," he assured himself.

Ultimately, the Chono reassembled the canoes on the opposite shore. They navigated the fractured spine of Chile by rowing through each channel until they encountered Chiloé Island on a gray June morning.

However, there was one final examination that remained.

In order to reach Chiloé, they were required to traverse an open gulf that was notorious for its colossal surges. The Chono cautioned them that this section of the ocean had eluded even Spanish vessels. However, they were unable to make a decision. They launched a canoe with the assistance of Martin and a temporary sail constructed from shredded blankets.

The snowfall commenced. The canoe experienced a malfunction. While Cheap murmured into the wind, Byron bailed water with his frozen hands. The sea trembled beneath them as they rowed through the pitch-black night. They eventually reached the island when dawn broke. Destroyed. Skeletal. Additionally, it is alive.

Cheap was virtually extinct. His mind had been irreparably damaged. He failed to identify himself or his cohorts. His body was infested with parasites, and his beard cascaded down like that of a hermit. His torso wasn't much more than skin that was stretched over bone, and his legs were distended to grotesque proportions. Byron could only liken him to "an anthill," which was crawling with mortality.

However, salvation once more arrived.

They were greeted by an indigenous village that provided them with sustenance and fire. "They constructed a bed of sheepskins for Captain Cheap," Byron wrote, "and, in fact, he would not have survived if it had not been for the generous assistance he now received."

They abided, recuperated. Drunk barley liquor. Consumed poultry. They laughed for the first time in a year. Campbell wrote, "We all enjoyed ourselves." "We believed that we were once again in the realm of the living." Byron, who had reached the age of eighteen during the ordeal, was no longer resembling a child or a man; rather, he was a spirit that had been shaped by ice, hunger, and fire.

Then, just as life appeared to be regaining momentum, fate struck once more.

As they advanced toward an additional village, Spanish soldiers emerged—uniformed phantoms that sliced through the forest. The castaways, who had endured shipwreck, mutiny, starvation, and lunacy, were now subjected to custody.

Their tale was not yet concluded. However, the reckoning had already commenced.

Captain David Cheap would later write, his words etched with humiliation, "I was now reduced to the infamous necessity of surrendering myself." He regarded it as the "most severe misfortune that can befall a man." Upon receiving a formal declaration of submission to the Spanish Crown from Spanish authorities in exchange for sustenance, he refused and threw the document to the ground in disgust. He declared, "The officers of the King of England could die of hunger, but they abhorred to beg."

It was of no consequence. Although his pride was tattered, it was unable to generate an escape route. Cheap and the remaining castaways—Byron, Hamilton, and Campbell—were transported to Valparaíso, a port city on the Chilean mainland, as there was no other avenue for advancement. They were thrown into the "condemned hole," a prison that was so dim that they were unable to see one another's features. "There were only four bare walls," Byron recollected. Additionally, a parasite epidemic ensued.

The residents perceived them as both an enemy and an object of curiosity. Crowds gathered to observe the Englishmen who had been apprehended. Sensing an opportunity for profit, the guards led the prisoners out and paraded them like exotic animals, charging onlookers to observe their hollowed forms. Byron wrote bitterly, "The soldiers made a pretty penny." "For the sake of the spectacle, they extracted money from each individual."

The four inmates were relocated to Santiago after a seven-month period. Their fortunes underwent a significant change in that location. The governor granted them parole, acknowledging their status as both captives of war and gentlemen. They were permitted to reside outside the prison fortifications as long as they refrained from engaging with the British.

Their time in Santiago was spent in an unusual state of suspended animation. One evening, they dined with Don José Pizarro, the Spanish admiral who had previously pursued Anson's fleet across the globe. During a somber exchange of war tales, Pizarro disclosed that his own expedition had been completely decimated, with his ships being torn apart by the fury of Cape Horn. A single vessel, which was carrying five hundred individuals, had disappeared entirely. Another individual, who was carrying seven hundred, had fallen. The remainder had been compelled to retreat due to malnutrition, mutiny, and despair. Rats were sold by sailors for four dollars each. Before retreating in shame, Pizarro had personally executed mutineers. It was difficult to determine whether his defeat or Anson's anguish was more severe. The ocean had not spared any side.

Cheap and his men were isolated in a country that was not their own, despite their gentler captivity. "Each day here seems to last an eternity," Cheap deplored. However, nearly three years after their captivity, news arrived that hostilities had ceased, and Britain and Spain had reached an agreement to exchange prisoners.

Hamilton, Byron, and Cheap were granted permission to depart. Cheap referred to them as "my two faithful companions and fellow sufferers." However, Campbell, who was once one of the most loyal, remained behind. He had become excessively close to the Spanish, and it is possible that he had even converted to Catholicism, as per Cheap. The implication was damning. If accurate, it would imply that each grave offense enumerated in the Articles of War had been committed by a member of the Wager crew. Treason is included.

The trio passed the spectral contours of Wager Island, the site that had broken them, as they set sail for England once more. They retraced the path of their ruin as they rounded Cape Horn, which was now silent and almost taunting in its tranquility. Their reluctant escort home was the sea that had once been their jailer.

By the time they arrived at Dover, Byron, who was then twenty-two years old, had borrowed a horse and was galloping toward London. He ignored the shouts of the gatekeepers as he sped past them, dressed in tattered clothing and without a coin for tolls. "I was compelled to defraud," he acknowledged, "by riding as hard as I could, without giving the slightest consideration to the men who called out to stop me."

He traversed fields and thatched hamlets before entering the sprawl of Europe's greatest city. In his absence, London had expanded, with 700,000 individuals residing in brick townhouses, tenement slums, vibrant markets, and carriage-clogged lanes. It was the heart of an empire, pulsing with commerce and conquest, oblivious to the ghosts it had left behind.

Byron arrived at Great Marlborough Street and approached the residence where he had last seen his companions and family. Boarded up. The world had undergone a transformation, and no one had informed him. He wrote, "I was unaware of who was alive, who was deceased, or where to proceed."

He discovered a dry-goods establishment that his family had previously frequented while wandering through the city. From there, he discovered that his sister Isabella, who was once an adolescent and is now a married noblewoman, resided in the vicinity of Soho Square. He hastily arrived at the address, knocked on the door, and was met by a suspicious porter. Byron was adamant. The attendant conceded.

Isabella was situated within. Composed, refined, and thin. A woman who had authored volumes on etiquette was now confronted with a ragged stranger who claimed her blood. She conducted an examination of him. Afterward, acknowledgment ensued.

Byron wrote, "My sister received me with such joy and surprise." She had kissed the boy farewell, but he had vanished. A man, sculpted by fire, frost, and fate, stood before her.

David Cheap was no longer the captain who had stood stiff-backed on the quarterdeck of the Wager, shouting orders into the icy spray. Upon his arrival in London, he was approaching fifty years old and had been hollowed out by captivity, disease, and the spirits that had pursued him ever since the ship had shattered on the rocks. He had obsessively relived each moment of pandemonium, each betrayal, and each decision in his isolation. And now, he discovered that his name had already been dragged through the gutter—not in a formal charge, but in print.

John Bulkeley had authored a book.

Bulkeley, the Wager's gunner-turned-mutineer-turned-narrator, depicted Cheap in A Voyage to the South Seas as not only incompetent but also homicidal—a man so consumed by pride and fury that he had become a threat to his own crew. Cheap's reputation could be irreparably damaged, and he may even be executed under the Articles of War if the Admiralty accepts the accusations.

In response, Cheap was extremely critical. In a letter to an Admiralty official, he denounced Bulkeley and his cohort as cowards and liars, stating, "For what can be expected of such poltroons... after most inhumanly abandoning us and destroying at their departure everything they thought could be of any use to us?" However, Cheap declined to respond with a competing publication. He was not interested in engaging in Grub Street duels or selling his honor for shillings. He would reserve his rendition for the sole forum that was significant—a court martial.

He provided a formal deposition to the Secretary of the Admiralty, claiming that "my conduct will appear unblameable both before and after our shipwreck" after the evidence was evaluated by his fellow commanding officers. He wrote coldly about Bulkeley, stating, "I have nothing to say for nor against the villains, until the day of trial." He added ominously that there would be nothing to prevent the full weight of justice from being served. Additionally, the gallows may be involved.

However, the streets of London were already ablaze with stories, particularly outside the corridors of power.

The press, which had recently been freed from censorship and was insatiable for scandal, fueled the fire. The Wager affair became the latest fixation of the Grub Street hacks, the tabloid scribes of the eighteenth century. Bulkley versus inexpensive. Defiance in contrast to discipline. Entropy versus empire. Bulkeley and his men had physically restrained Cheap and Hamilton, leaving them for "more merciful barbarians," as the Caledonian Mercury breathlessly reported. Hamilton was quoted by another periodical, which characterized Cheap as "mysterious... arrogant and high," although it also noted that he had acted with "sagacious foresight."

The pandemonium prompted publishers to act quickly in order to capitalize on it. Bulkeley's initial journal was the first to be introduced. Subsequently, Midshipman Campbell composed The Sequel, which was composed in a hasty frenzy to defend himself from accusations of treason upon his return from Chile shortly after Cheap. However, Campbell's motivations were uncertain. He fled England shortly after the publication and enlisted in the Spanish military. It was a narrative twist that would have been considered too improbable for a work of fiction.

John Byron, a naval officer who is currently ascending in rank and has his own aspirations, maintained a relatively low profile. Bulkeley's actions were described as "nothing less than direct mutiny" by him; however, he declined to publish a rebuttal. He perceived no benefit in engaging in what he termed "egotism."

Others were less circumspect. An Affecting Narrative of the Unfortunate Voyage and Catastrophe of His Majesty's Ship Wager, a pamphlet that was notably lurid, was purportedly based on "authentic journals." In reality, it was a preposterous plagiarism of Bulkeley's account, rewritten to glorify Cheap and uphold the Crown's authority. Bulkeley's own words had been transformed into a weapon against him, as scholar Philip Edwards later observed.

The truth became more difficult to ascertain amid the numerous conflicting voices—some of which were factual and others were fictitious. The narrative was subject to change based on the version that the reader selected. Bulkeley, who was once celebrated as a hero for guiding survivors home, now found his legacy being undermined by a deluge of embellished retellings and unauthorized editions. With each copy sold, his fury intensified.

The chaos was such that the Admiralty was unable to continue to disregard it.

A summons was issued within days of Cheap's return to English soil. It was disseminated throughout ports, nailed to tavern doorways, and published in newspapers. The Wager's remaining officers, petty officers, and mariners were summoned to Portsmouth for a comprehensive court martial. The legal process would commence within the next few weeks.

What lay ahead was not merely an ordeal. A reckoning was in order.

The council of judges would consist exclusively of naval commanders, including those who, like Cheap, had confronted rebellion and storms. Bulkeley's defiant journal, Cheap's restrained fury, Hamilton's evolving loyalty, Campbell's desertion, and Byron's haunted neutrality would all require the case to navigate a fog thick with contradiction. It would filter out biased retellings, disputed facts, and stories that have been repurposed to advance political agendas.

Janet Malcolm, a writer, once stated, "The law is the protector of the ideal of unmediated truth... stripped bare of the ornament of narration." However, the Wager's narrative was a narrative of descent, as it recounted the transformation of men of empire into mutineers, saviors, traitors, and animals in the most remote region of the world, even when its literary flourishes were removed. That issue could not be thoroughly resolved by any court. However, it would at least attempt to.

In doing so, it endangered to surpass even Anson's dazzling victory.

The Wager threatened to reveal what the galleon had gilded.

------- * * * -------

Chapter 24
THE DOCKET

John Bulkeley was in a modest London lodging, enjoying tea, when he received the notice that sealed his fate. The Admiralty had issued a court-martial summons to all surviving members of His Majesty's ship Wager. However, that was not the most severe aspect of the situation. He was promptly informed by a counsel that a warrant had been issued for his detention. A marshal was pursuing him in an unknown location within the city.

Bulkeley pursued the individual who was designated to apprehend him in a cruel twist of fate. He disguised himself as a relative of one of the longboat survivors and confronted the marshal with a disingenuous question: What would happen to the men who had successfully reached Brazil now that Captain Cheap had returned?

The marshal responded without hesitation, "Hanged."

"For god's sake, for what?" Bulkeley wept. "For avoiding drowning?" And has a perpetrator finally returned to serve as their accuser?

The marshal shook his head. "Sir, they have committed such atrocities against Captain Cheap while he was a prisoner that I am of the opinion that the gunner and carpenter will be hanged, if no one else."

Bulkeley then disclosed the truth: "I am the unfortunate gunner of the Wager."

The marshal was compelled to apprehend him due to his shock.

Bulkeley was detained while Lieutenant Baynes, the carpenter Cummins, and the boatswain King were apprehended—names that are inscribed into the narrative like scars. The marshal was instructed to "take particular care that the gunner and carpenter did not make their escape" after they were conveyed to Portsmouth together. HMS Prince George, a ninety-gun warship that towered over the estuary, was the vessel to which they were rowed and placed on board. They awaited judgment once more at sea, sequestered from the world.

Even letters from family members were rejected.

Byron, too, received his summons. He arrived voluntarily. Cheap voluntarily embarked on the Prince George, presumably relinquishing his sword in the process. He maintained his authoritative demeanor, despite his persistent respiratory illness and gout: his waistcoat was rigid with brass, his lips were tightly pursed, and his eyes were unwavering. They were reunited for the first time since the cursed island. Bulkeley had previously stated that each individual would "give account of his actions" and "allow justice to be served."

The Wager affair was no longer merely a scandal. It was now a challenge of naval law itself.

Although British naval justice was known for its brutal finality, the Articles of War permitted some degree of flexibility—at least at the parchment level. Depending on the circumstances, even capital offenses may be mitigated. However, the offenses associated with the Wager were not trivial infractions such as insubordination or napping on duty. They suggested a complete collapse: a crew that was torn apart by terror, pride, and desperation.

The legal facts were unambiguous. Bulkeley and his men had confined their commander and left him on the island. In the absence of a trial or warning, Cheap fatally shot a man named Cozens. These were not matters of interpretation; they were facts. Joseph Conrad once wrote that the law only required facts: "Facts! They demanded facts."

The allegations were piled on top of one another. Bulkeley, Baynes, and the others had the potential to violate:

Article 19: Death is the penalty for mutinous assembly.

Article 20: The concealment of mutinous designs.

Article 21: Striking or disputing with a superior officer.

Article 17: Desertion—also subject to death.

In the rigging, additional charges loomed like ghosts: cowardice, thievery, defiance of direct orders, and even irreligious conduct—"scandalous actions in derogation of God's honor.".

However, Cheap was also not secure. He was confronted with what may have been the most severe allegation of all: murder. The brutality of Article 28 of the Articles of War was evident: "All murders and willful killing...shall be punished with death." There is no clause. There is no discretion. Cozens were not equipped. He had passed away without a cause, without a trial, and without a final statement.

Even Byron, who was moderate and loyal, was unable to find peace. He had momentarily mutinied when he fled with Bulkeley's group, but he later returned. Would the court consider his return as a form of redemption? Alternatively, would they only observe the desertion?

All parties had endeavored to safeguard themselves through the use of paper: meticulously crafted journals, sworn depositions, and edited recollections. However, the court would not be influenced by literary grace or omission. Additionally, the legal documents that Bulkeley and his colleagues wrote during the expedition—documents that they believed would safeguard them—only served to confirm that they had been aware of the regulations from the outset. and intentionally violated them.

The purpose of a naval court-martial was not limited to determining culpability or innocence. It was theater—state theater—with an audience of monarchs, commanders, and mariners. It was constructed to instill fear and bolster the empire's authority. The process was designed to "convey the majesty and strength of the state," as one scholar put it, and to cause seafarers to tremble at the prospect that their lives could be terminated by rope, rather than by tempest or cannon.

The risks were not hypothetical. In the aftermath of the mutiny on HMS Bounty in 1789, the Admiralty pursued the perpetrators worldwide. Those who were deemed guilty were executed on deck in the presence of a silent, assembled crew. Yellow flags were hoisted. Nooses were manipulated. Their corpses remained suspended for hours, serving as a warning to all sailors in attendance, as they were buffeted by the breeze.

The men of the Wager were now awaiting the Prince George, uncertain as to whether their fate would resemble that gruesome spectacle.

On a Sunday, they convened for a shipboard service. The chaplain's voice reverberated across the timbers, as he declared that the sea had the power to soften a man's heart. He also cautioned those in attendance to relinquish any "vain notions or expectations of a reprieve or pardon."

The atmosphere was tranquil. The males maintained their silence. The sea, their venerable confessor, awaited.

They had endured betrayal, madness, starvation, and shipwreck.

Currently, it is possible that they would not endure the legal process.

------- * * * -------

Chapter 25
THE COURT-MARTIAL

The Prince George, a ninety-gun man-of-war that was anchored in Portsmouth harbor on the morning of April 15, 1746, stood motionless and gleaming in ceremonial readiness. The decks had been cleansed until they shone like bone. The rigging was taut, the weapons were rolled out in rigid formation, and the hammocks were stowed in perfect rows. At the masthead, a Union Jack was raised. Then a single cannon was fired, serving as a signal of justice rather than combat.

The Wager survivors' court-martial had commenced.

Frederick Marryat, a naval novelist who would later join the Royal Navy, once stated that such trials were intended to "strike the mind with awe—even of a captain himself." The full theatrical force of military authority was now on exhibit. The ship's grand cabin had been converted into a floating courtroom, featuring a long table draped in green cloth, pens, inkwells, paper, prayer books, and—most ominously—the Articles of War.

Sir James Steuart, vice-admiral and commander-in-chief of all His Majesty's ships at Portsmouth, presided over the thirteen justices who ascended the deck. Steuart presided with the same solemnity as a man who possessed the authority to sentence individuals to death at the age of nearly seventy. The other assessors, who were captains and commodores, were not unfamiliar with command or combat. They appeared to be more akin to Captain David Cheap's contemporaries than to the gunner John Bulkeley and his motley crew. However, naval tribunals were identified as punishing their own. Admiral John Byng would be executed less than a decade later for neglecting to "do his utmost" in battle. This act was so controversial that it would prompt Voltaire to jest that the English "shoot an admiral from time to time to encourage the others."

Currently, the fate of Cheap was uncertain.

Despite the fact that George Anson was not present at the trial, his influence was significant. Anson, who was previously a commodore and is now a rising figure on the Board of Admiralty, had advocated for Cheap's appointment and had promoted numerous surviving officers of the squadron. He was the leader of the expedition that captured the Spanish galleon and returned home as a hero. However, the individual whom he had previously appointed as the Wager's commander was being investigated for murder. Anson received a letter from Cheap that was a combination of congratulation and appeal. Cheap had written, "I must implore your favor and protection, which I am confident I will receive provided that I conduct myself in a manner that is commensurate with my duties. Conversely, I shall anticipate neither when I behave in a manner that is contrary to my obligations." Anson, who was consistently cautious, conveyed his ongoing support for Cheap's family.

The defendants were presented to the court. They would speak for themselves, as was customary; no attorneys were present. However, they were allowed to summon witnesses and cross-examine others. The charges against them were frustratingly imprecise, despite the fact that they had already submitted official statements of fact.

Bulkeley maintained his usual defiant demeanor. He protested when requested to provide his deposition regarding the Wager's wreckage, stating, "I have always believed, or at least the laws of my country dictate, that a man must be accused when he is a prisoner." He lamented that he was unaware of the reasons for his trial. "What is the most effective method for preparing a defense?"

He was informed that he only needed to address the cause of the catastrophe.

Consequently, the trial commenced.

The initial contact was made to Cheap. He only pointed his finger once at Lieutenant Baynes in relation to the Wager's loss, alleging that he neglected to notify him that land had been sighted the day before the ship collided with the rocks. The judge inquired, "Do you charge any officer, in addition to the lieutenant, with any degree of accessory to the Wager's loss?"

"No, sir," Cheap replied. "I absolve them of all of that."

His other allegations, including attempted murder, desertion, and mutiny, were not addressed. The trial's scope had already been reduced.

Next, Bulkeley arrived. The judges inquired as to why he had not lowered the anchor prior to the ship's grounding. He replied, "The cable was foul." Bulkeley, whose published journal had excoriated Cheap, paused when asked whether he had any objections to the conduct of the captain or officers.

"I am unable to accuse any officer," he stated.

The words were overshadowed by the silence. There was evidently a bargain at hand.

The remaining castaways were summoned one by one.

Carpenter Cummins, who had previously accused Cheap of causing the accident and had written about him as a murderer, responded with a composed "No" when asked whether the captain had neglected his responsibilities.

Boatswain King, a man who had stolen liquor, assaulted Cheap, and worn officers' attire as a costume, responded, "The captain behaved very well." Personally, I have no complaints regarding him or any other officer.

Even Byron, whose private memories were replete with horror, was only questioned about the ship's rigging and dismissed without reference to the nightmare that ensued after the disaster.

Baynes was the sole individual who was officially charged. He asserted that he had failed to report the sighting of land because he had mistaken it for clouds.

The justices resumed their duties following a brief recess.

The decision was unanimous.

The court declared that Captain David Cheap had fulfilled his obligation and employed all available methods to safeguard His Majesty's Ship Wager while under his command. All other officers and crew members were exonerated, with the exception of Baynes, who received only a mild reprimand.

The trial concluded.

Bulkeley was overjoyed. He wrote, "We witnessed the great and glorious power of the Almighty in advocating for our cause and protecting us from the violence of men." He declared himself "honorably acquitted."

Cheap, who had been yearning for revenge and vindication for an extended period, was ultimately unsuccessful. He had been spared punishment, but he had also been denied justice. He continued to serve as a commander; however, the aura of authority that had once enveloped him had diminished. His adversaries were granted freedom. His grievances were never addressed. And the truth, if it had ever existed in a single, unambiguous form, was left to decay between competing accounts, concealed beneath layers of silence.

In the end, the law required evidence. However, what it received were omissions, bargains, and decorum. Protocol had swallowed the truths that had once bled across sand and deck.

Discipline was maintained by the court.

However, this is not the case.

No additional accusations were filed. Mutiny was not prosecuted. No one was found guilty of homicide. The court-martial aboard HMS Prince George concluded with a breathless anticlimax, as the austere ritual, cannon-shot opening, and thirteen uniformed judges ultimately served a decision to do nothing more.

Captain David Cheap would not be prosecuted for the slaying of Midshipman Cozens. John Bulkeley and his followers would not be prosecuted for the abandonment of their commanding officer, desertion, or mutiny. The Admiralty had no intention of conducting any additional investigations.

Officials relied on a technicality—an obscure clause concealed within the naval regulations—to substantiate this extraordinary silence. They asserted that mariners were no longer entitled to wages following a shipwreck. Consequently, the sailors of the Wager could have reasonably inferred that they were no longer subject to naval law. According to historian Glyndwr Williams, it was a "escape clause"—convenient, opaque, and profoundly flawed. The same regulations explicitly stipulated that seamen's pay and obligations would continue as long as they were still able to recover provisions from the disaster. The Wager had produced sails, containers of food, powder, and weapons. The warriors had not only survived, but they had also assumed control.

The Admiralty's refusal to prosecute charges bore "an uncomfortable whiff of justification," according to Rear Admiral C. H. Layman, an authority on the case. The memory of a collapse that was so complete and so shameful that it threatened the myth of Britain itself was not merely testimony; it was buried.

That caution was due to a valid reason.

The central illusion of British imperial power, which was that its officers were men of moral authority, discipline, and civility, was shattered by the revelation of the truth about the events that transpired on Wager Island—the drunkenness, the thefts, the beatings, the muttered plots, and the murder. The control of Britannia was not based on bloodshed, but rather on reason. But if the truth had been revealed in court, it would have been far less flattering: that the empire was not solely constructed by explorers and admirals, but by fearful men in rags, crawling through mud with daggers in their belts.

However, the Admiralty's desire to ignore was not limited to the Wager.

The War of Jenkins' Ear, which was initiated with the guise of honor and indignation, was, in numerous respects, a catastrophe. Admiral Edward Vernon led nearly 200 ships in an assault on the Spanish stronghold of Cartagena in 1741. Bureaucratic incompetence, infighting, and disease ultimately led to the campaign's demise. Vernon bid a somber farewell after 67 days and more than 10,000 British fatalities, stating, "We are enveloped in the toils of death." He then issued an order for a retreat.

Even Anson's expedition, which was celebrated for its capturing of the Covadonga, had its own shadow. More than 1,300 of the 1,955 individuals who had embarked on the voyage perished. Indeed, Anson returned with a treasure valued at £400,000. But the British public had incurred a loss of more than £43 million as a result of the conflict. A acrimonious poem that was published in a London paper that was dissenting in nature posed the following question:

Britons who are deceived! Consequently, why should you gloat of a treasure that was acquired at a triple price?

... Think of the great mischief it has caused, The unprofitable loss of Albion's sons.

The reality was that Britain had shed blood in pursuit of gold.

Additionally, the conflict had been initiated under false pretenses. Spanish forces purportedly severed the ear of a merchant commander named Robert Jenkins in 1731. The incident received minimal attention until seven years later, when war-hungry politicians resurrected it and wielded it as a banner. Legend has it that Jenkins removed his severed ear from a container when he appeared before the House of Commons in 1738. However, there is no official record. According to certain scholars, he was never present. Edmund Burke would subsequently refer to it as "the fable of Jenkins's ear."

Profit was the primary motivator behind the conflict.

The British South Sea Company was granted an asiento in 1713, which authorized the company to supply Spain's American colonies with up to 4,800 enslaved Africans annually. The agreement, which was portrayed as a diplomatic triumph, facilitated the entry of British merchants into the Americas with contraband, including slaves, sugar, and textiles. British merchants expressed their dissatisfaction with Spain's enforcement of anti-smuggling laws. The clamor for war intensified. The public was never informed that the war had commenced in part to safeguard the right to sell human beings, despite the fact that it was roused by discussions of national honor.

The War of Jenkins' Ear had already been incorporated into a broader geopolitical storm—the War of the Austrian Succession, a contest of empires—by the time the Wager court-martial discreetly closed in 1746. In the subsequent century, Britain's navy would achieve successive victories, thereby transforming the island kingdom into what James Thomson referred to as the "empire of the deep." In 1913, Great Britain governed more than 400 million individuals across a quarter of the Earth's landmass.

However, the empire was still susceptible in 1746. It was unable to tolerate mutiny.

History has demonstrated the consequences of a mutiny that is too perilous to be identified. French soldiers declined to charge into certain destruction during the First World War. The government referred to the rebellion as a "Rectification of Morale" rather than acknowledging it. Files were guarded for fifty years.

The Wager incident adhered to the same pattern. A mutiny would not be officially acknowledged. There will be no disciplinary action. There was no investigation into the process by which British officers evolved into animals. The court-martial files were devoid of Cheap's complete deposition, which included his allegations of murder, cowardice, and duplicity. Witness accounts were never verified. The documents were never reopened.

The record, as it was preserved, recounted a different narrative: a ship that was lost at sea. A formality trial. A few inquiries. A few modest acquittals. Reprimand for a single officer.

Silence ensued.

In the annals of British history, the Wager's descent into savagery was subsequently referred to as "the mutiny that never was" by Glyndwr Williams.

------- * * * -------

Chapter 26
THE VERSION THAT WON

A new chapter emerged three months after the final gavel fell in the Wager court-martial, a proceeding that was so meticulously confined that it had absolved nearly everyone and revealed almost nothing. Not located in London. Not from any judge or admiral. But from the sea itself, in the guise of three ragged men who staggered off a ship in Portsmouth in the summer of 1746.

They were survivors of Bulkeley's longboat expedition, men who were presumed to be deceased, lost to the passage of time and the ocean. Midshipman Isaac Morris was one of them. His return would not only revive the Wager narrative, but also reveal another tale that had been concealed in the tide: a second mutiny. One that the British Empire had neither orchestrated nor silenced, as it had transpired in a location remote from courtrooms, on a vessel that was not its own, and was commanded by enslaved men, indigenous warriors who fought with nothing but knives, rope, and fury.

Morris's ordeal had commenced on a shore in southern Patagonia over four years prior. He and seven others had landed from the Speedwell in order to search for food. Subsequently, the breezes altered. The rudder was damaged. And Bulkeley, along with his remaining crew, sailed away.

Bulkeley's party hurled a barrel containing gunpowder and a note of explanation over the departing deck. Morris and his companions collapsed to their knees on the sand as they observed their salvation disappear into the horizon. Later, he referred to the abandonment as "the most heinous act of cruelty."

They had already been castaways for eight months prior to that. In his own words, they were now "fatigued, sickly, and devoid of provisions" in a wilderness that provided nothing for free. Tragically, four of the soldiers perished. Morris and three others maintained their survival by foraging for berries, snaring wild animals, and consuming rainwater.

They made a desperate attempt to reach Buenos Aires, which is located hundreds of miles to the north, but they were unable to do so. Subsequently, a peculiar noise was heard: hooves. Morris turned toward the hammering and prepared himself for death. Rather, deliverance arrived on horseback. They were discovered by a group of indigenous Patagonians, who, to their surprise, treated them with benevolence. They slaughtered a horse for meat, lighted a fire, and provided the men with pieces of old blankets to conceal their nakedness. Morris wrote, "They treated us with exceptional humanity." The strangers possessed a higher level of respect than the mariners who had abandoned them to decay.

For months, the castaways were led from village to village. Then, in May 1744, they arrived in Buenos Aires, two and a half years after being marooned. However, liberation was a mere illusion. They were incarcerated by the Spanish.

They were detained for more than a year before being transferred to a substantial warship, which was equipped with sixty-six cannons and nearly five hundred sailors, for transportation to Spain. The skipper of the vessel? None other than Don José Pizarro, the same officer who had previously pursued Anson across the Pacific. Eleven enslaved indigenous males, including a chief named Orellana, were aboard the vessel in addition to the British prisoners.

A brutal Spanish raid had captured Orellana and his soldiers just months prior. They belonged to a tribe located near Buenos Aires that had long opposed colonization. Presently, they were compelled to perform manual labor while chained to the ship. The beatings, the lashings, and the senseless cruelty were subsequently described by Morris and his fellow survivors in their testimonies. The Spanish commanders subjected Orellana and his men to whippings on the slightest pretext, occasionally for amusement and occasionally to establish their authority.

One day, Orellana was instructed to ascend the mast. He declined. His punishment was swift; he was subjected to physical abuse until he collapsed, leaving him disoriented and bloodied.

Subsequently, on the third night of the voyage, an incident occurred.

Morris was the first to hear the pandemonium, which consisted of a thunderous sound of footsteps, a shout, and a crack, from below decks. Upon reaching the summit of the ladder, one of his companions fled to investigate and was fatally struck. When Morris ascended, he observed a Spanish soldier's body already on the deck. Then another. Then, he shouts out, "A mutiny! A mutiny!"

However, this was not a British matter. There are no officers. Uniforms are not required. Absence of Articles of War.

Orellana and his ten men had ascended.

They entered the quarterdeck without firearms, relying solely on blades that they had concealed and slingshots that they had constructed from scrap and rope. Spanish officers fled in a panic. Pizarro and his lieutenants fortified themselves in a cabin, extinguishing lamps and concealing themselves in the darkness. Meanwhile, others either retreated into the rigging or withdrew into the livestock pens located beneath the deck. Morris stood in amazement. A ship with a crew of five hundred and sixty-six cannons had been commandeered by eleven enslaved men.

The rebellion persisted for two hours.

It was one of the hundreds—possibly thousands—of indigenous uprisings and slave revolts that had etched a mark on the map of empire. According to historian Jill Lepore, these individuals had "revolted repeatedly," consistently questioning the legitimacy of their rule.

However, the insurrection aboard Pizarro's warship, like so many others, would culminate in violence.

Pizarro's men, who were confined to the cabin, lowered a bucket into the powder chamber by means of a rope. The gunner refilled it with ammunition. The officers finally broke through the door, armed with their weapons. Orellana stood in the moonlight, nearly naked, having shed the Western attire that had been imposed upon him. The night air caused his chest to heave as he inhaled profoundly.

Afterward, the officers discharged their firearms.

Orellana was wounded by a bullet. He fell and staggered. A pool of his blood was observed on the deck. Morris would later assist in the compilation of a report that would explicitly assert, "The insurrection was quelled."

However, the narrative did not conclude at that point.

Orellana's remaining samurai fled to the railings as the officers reclaimed the ship. They issued one final lament and jumped into the sea, without uttering a word or resorting to pleas. Death was the preferred option for each of them, as opposed to servitude.

They disappeared beneath the waters.

Their identities would not be published in England. Their rebellion would not be assessed by a court-martial, examined by admiralty attorneys, or commemorated in any royal dispatch. It was not included in the official record.

However, it was a mutiny that was more definitive, courageous, and authentic than the one that the Wager's officers had made a concerted effort to eradicate.

The Wager affair would be remembered, if at all, as the scandal that never erupted. However, on a Spanish ship, a brief, audacious, and righteous rebellion erupted under a moonlit deck, and was subsequently drowned.

These eleven individuals lack a voice in a society that asserts the rule of law. However, for a brief period, they had occupied the quarterdeck.

At that time, they were in control.

Isaac Morris followed in the footsteps of numerous other survivors of the Wager affair by publishing a book upon his return to England. His forty-eight-page narrative was a valuable addition to the expanding collection of firsthand accounts authored by men who had barely escaped betrayal, lunacy, or starvation. The Wager, a shipwreck that had evolved into something more, was further enriched by each tale, which added a new layer to the sprawling narrative. This mirror, which was fractured and fogged by survival, reflected the workings of empire.

However, the individuals who recounted these narratives, including Morris, seldom perceived themselves as imperial agents. They did not discuss global trade or conquest; rather, they discussed the tasks of rigging sails, pursuing promotions, and scrounging together wages to send home. Their loyalty, if any, was to their messmates, the watch bell rhythms, the grog ration, and the dim prospect of prize money. However, it was precisely this unthinking complicity—the daily routine of duty without question—that maintained the British Empire. It did not necessitate visionaries. It necessitated mariners, survivors, and laborers. Males who persevered and submitted.

Nevertheless, one individual was never granted a voice. Not in any journal, not in a courtroom deposition, not even in a letter.

Just as Morris survived the wilderness, John Duck, the free Black seaman who had come onshore with Morris's abandoned party, did as well. He persevered through the solitude, the hunger, and the cold. He arrived at the periphery of Buenos Aires. However, his narrative diverged from the others at that point. He was apprehended and enslaved. Morris never encountered him again.

"I am of the opinion that he will conclude his life in bondage." Morris wrote with a grim expression, "there being no prospect of his ever returning to England."

Duck's narrative, like that of innumerable others, was rendered unrecognizable by silence, rather than by fire or storm. The archives' silence, which never captured his testimony. The silence of an empire that refused to commemorate the enslaved within its ranks, let alone those who were abducted into slavery after serving under the Union Jack.

As imperial history progressed, those silences served as the foundation for the construction of more triumphant and noisier narratives.

By 1746, a novel form of competition had emerged—not over territory or ships, but over narrative. Who would be responsible for the official narrative of Anson's expedition? Who would assert that Britain's most significant contemporary maritime expedition was composed by them?

Richard Walter, the Centurion's chaplain, asserted his claim at an early stage. He discreetly commenced the production of an official chronicle, despite Pascoe Thomas, the schoolmaster of the ship, accusing him of attempting to monopolize the narrative. Thomas was the first to publish A True and Impartial Journal of a Voyage to the South-Seas in 1745. An additional account, which was likely composed by a Grub Street ghostwriter, praised Anson's expedition as "undoubtedly of the greatest worth and importance."

However, the definitive version was Reverend Walter's book, A Voyage Round the World in the Years 1740–1744, which was published in 1748.

The book is a sweeping, high-stakes narrative of survival and triumph, spanning nearly 400 pages and featuring finely detailed sketches from a Centurion lieutenant. Yes, the prose was stilted and occasionally bland due to the logbook minutiae, but the drama was compelling. Anson was depicted as a hero who embodied courage and fortitude. Only briefly— and meticulously—was the Wager affair addressed. The book asserted that Cheap had made every effort to save his troops, and the shooting of Cozens was entirely justified. It was asserted that the company had erroneously believed that the shipwreck rendered naval hierarchy obsolete.

It was an exceptional example of narrative management.

It is peculiar that the book provides a clergyman's perspective on God, yet it scarcely mentions Him. Walter had not been present during the Centurion's intense combat with the galleon, as he had already departed from China prior to the engagement, despite the fact that the first-person narrator described the event. Subsequent investigations revealed the truth: Walter was not the solitary author. Benjamin Robins, a mathematician and pamphleteer, had ghostwritten a significant portion of the prose.

However, George Anson was the true architect behind it all.

The endeavor was meticulously curated by Anson, despite his assertion that he had a "aversion to writing." Source materials were furnished by him. Walter was his choice. Robins was purportedly compensated £1,000 to develop the narrative. He authorized each and every aspect, including the illustrations. The British victory was rendered even more extraordinary by the manipulation of the image of the Centurion's combat, which increased the size of the Spanish galleon.

Anson's objective was not solely to be remembered. He desired for the Empire to be remembered through him.

The book commenced with a comprehensive assertion of Britain's "manifest superiority... in commerce and glory" and concluded with a glowing endorsement of perseverance in the face of adversity. It illustrated Anson as a man who was composed in the face of adversity, benevolent toward his troops, and honorable in all of his decisions. The Wager wreck was reduced to a trivial incident—an unfortunate storm that occurred during an otherwise commendable voyage.

The narrative exceeded all expectations.

It was a bestseller, translated into numerous languages, and widely read throughout Europe and its colonies. Rousseau referred to Anson as a "grand homme." A thorough summary was composed by Montesquieu. Captain James Cook traveled with a duplicate on the Endeavour. It was loaded onto the Beagle by Charles Darwin. Anson's Voyage was the quintessential maritime adventure of the British imagination for a century.

Critics described it as "a classic adventure story," "one of the most enjoyable small books in the world's library," and "the most popular travel book of its era."

And as a result, Britain discovered the narrative it desired to convey. Mutiny is not a factor. Not of homicide. Not due to starvation, betrayal, or the sale of a Black seaman into slavery. However, endurance is a virtue. Of splendor. The calm, righteous hand of the empire that guided it through peril.

It was not the most accurate account.

However, it proved to be the most advantageous.

The British Empire had discovered its myth of the sea in the aftermath of the wreckage, following the bloodshed, silence, and distorted truths.

------- * * * -------

Epilogue

Ultimately, the Wager's men continued to exist as if the events of their past had never occurred. It was as though the island, the gunfire, the hunger, the mutiny, and the silence that ensued were all components of a dark collective dream that the sea had swept away.

Captain David Cheap, whose reputation had previously been on the brink of oblivion, was reinstated with dignity. He was granted command of a forty-four-gun warship with Admiral Anson's assistance. He observed a Spanish vessel while sailing off Madeira on Christmas Day, 1746, just eight months after the court-martial. This time, there was no desertion or mutiny. He stood erect on the quarterdeck, issuing commands, his guns loaded, and his pride redeemed. Subsequently, he informed the Admiralty that the enemy vessel had been captured within "half an hour." More than one hundred silver containers were present on the vessel. Cheap had finally claimed the prize he referred to as "so valuable."

He retired shortly thereafter, having recently married, acquired fortune, and become the proprietor of a Scottish estate. However, the past declined to be laid to rest. The London newspapers served as a reminder of the incident that had followed him like a specter when he passed away in 1752 at the age of fifty-nine. One obituary observed that "he fatally shot one man on the spot" after being shipwrecked.

Many others vanished into more tranquil circumstances. John Bulkeley, who was always resourceful, sailed to a land where reinvention was feasible—America. He relocated to Pennsylvania, the future site of the revolution, and reissued his narrative in 1757. Morris's accusation that he had abandoned his troops was omitted from this edition. After that, Bulkeley disappeared. His final words in print referred to America as "the Garden of the Lord," a land where transgressions could be forgotten—if not forgiven.

John Byron elected to pursue an alternative course of study. He remained in the Royal Navy for more than two decades, eventually achieving the rank of Vice-Admiral. In 1764, he was tasked with leading a circumnavigation of the globe, a feat that Anson had previously accomplished. A grim irony was included in his orders: to explore the coasts of Patagonia for any Wager castaways who might still be clinging to life. He was unsuccessful in his search.

Byron successfully concluded the voyage without incurring any losses; however, storms ensued in every location where he traveled. Foul-Weather Jack became a nickname among sailors. Nevertheless, his men held him in high regard, not for his good fortune, but for a more uncommon quality: compassion. "A man who was extremely unfortunate," wrote one biographer, "but a brave and excellent officer." Byron may have discovered a calm redemption in the storm-tossed masts and heaving decks, as the community that had failed on Wager Island was reborn in fellowship at sea.

He maintained his confidentiality. He did not elaborate on the cannibalism, the gunshot, the dog that was consumed, or the sanity that prevailed among the starving men. However, The Narrative of the Honourable John Byron was ultimately published in 1768, a considerable amount of time after Cheap's death. He wrote candidly of his former captain's "rash and hasty" conduct, now that he was no longer bound by loyalty or fear. Marine Lieutenant Hamilton, Cheap's final staunch advocate, was incensed and accused Byron of a "significant injustice." However, the book was commended for its honesty and pathos, as well as its "simple, affecting, and romantic" tone. It would not alter the course of history; however, it would alter the course of a life.

That existence belonged to Lord Byron, the poet, Byron's grandson, who never encountered his grandfather but was captivated by his narrative. He would compose the following in Don Juan:

"The fate of our grandfather from the past was reversed for me— He was unable to rest at sea, and I was unable to rest on land."

As for Admiral George Anson, the empire's chosen champion, his legacy continued to flourish. An entire French fleet was captured by him during the War of the Austrian Succession. However, his most significant accomplishment was not achieved on the water; rather, it was achieved through the application of paper and policy. He dedicated two decades to the professionalization of the Royal Navy, the establishment of a permanent marine corps, and the correction of the failings that had caused the Wager to fail. He was acclaimed as the "Father of the British Navy" as a result. He was the subject of the naming of several towns. John Byron even named his son George Anson Byron in honor of the man whose name had endured through every tempest.

However, legends are not impermanent.

The Centurion, the formidable vessel that had transported Anson's treasure home, was ultimately decommissioned. The lion's head figure was presented to a nobleman, exhibited at an inn, and subsequently relocated to Greenwich Hospital at the king's request. However, its significance diminished as time progressed. The lion was abandoned in a shed, where it decayed to an unrecognizable state.

Occasionally, an individual revisited the Wager incident.

Herman Melville observed in White-Jacket in 1850 that the castaways' narratives were an ideal choice for a tempestuous March evening. Patrick O'Brian transformed the narrative into a novel, The Unknown Shore, in 1959. This preliminary draft would subsequently serve as the foundation for his celebrated sea series.

However, the public failed to remember.

Currently, the Golfo de Penas is essentially unrecognized on nautical charts. Smith, Hertford, Crosslet, and Hobbs are the names of a few islands in close proximity to the northern headlands. These four marines were left behind on the shoreline when the final boat departed. Before dissipating into the sea and fog, they had shouted out, "God bless the King."

The geography of decisions is marked by Canal Cheap and Byron Island—one man who remained and one who returned. However, there are no longer any travelers who are aware of those names.

The Chono and Kawésqar, also known as the nomads of the sea, have vanished. Their destruction was precipitated by their encounter with Europeans. In a coastal hamlet located south of the Golfo de Penas, only a handful of Kawésqar remained by the early twentieth century.

Wager Island continues to endure, enveloped in solitude and sleet, despite the wind that batters it. The forests of the region are contorted and scorched by lightning. The craggy slopes of Mount Anson are enveloped in a near-perpetual mist that gradually descends to the littoral, resembling smoke. Celery continues to flourish in the vicinity of Mount Misery, and limpets continue to adhere to rocks, as they did during the time when the castaways foraged for them in order to survive.

And inland, planks that are half-buried in an icy stream, pierced with treenails, are slowly being consumed by time. These planks are five yards in length. The final remnants of His Majesty's Ship, the Wager.

Nothing else remains from the events that transpired there. There is no indication of the court martial. There is no monument to the soldiers who either died or mutinied. There is no record of Cozens's blood. I have no recollection of John Duck, who was sold into servitude.

Silence, wood, and moisture are the sole remaining elements.

Additionally, the understanding that empires do not perish in the presence of thunder.

They dissipate into the fog, one plank at a time.

------- * * * -------

Printed in Great Britain
by Amazon